Tears In A Bottle...

LESSONS FROM A BROKEN HEART

Joe Knight

TEARS IN A BOTTLE... Lessons from A Broken Heart *SECOND EDITION*

ISBN 978-1-947153-12-7

Layout by Rachel Greene, elfinpen.com

To Shaunda, Jodi, Lynn, Joey, Brian, Makenna, Keegan, Nora, and Joe the Third—and any other blessings to come.

Here's to many more Christmases and to never taking a single moment for granted.

Contents

Foreword...

By Rick BLUE
Former Pastor, Family Fellowship of Greenville. (retired)

I first met Joe Knight at a time of great need in both of our lives and ministries. Joe was about to be released from his position as worship leader in his church, through no fault of his own; and I was in desperate need of a worship leader, through some fault of my own. There is no doubt in my mind that God brought us together at the perfect time in both of our lives. We began a working relationship that developed into a deep and abiding friendship. Joe has always called me "Boss" out of great respect, but he didn't work for me. He worked with me.

As you will discover early in the pages of this book, I helped to engineer a meeting between Joe and the woman that I thought would make a perfect and wonderful wife for Joe. I was right! But that meeting would set in motion the chain of events that would ultimately lead to the writing of this book.

I love Joe Knight like David loved Jonathan. We have shared many a storm, and many more blessings together as we worked side by side. Though I am now retired as pastor of Family Fellowship, Joe still calls me "Boss." Well, the boss wept openly as I read this manuscript, and relived the story that so touched all of us at Family Fellowship Church. No doubt it will touch your heart as well.

Introduction...

I'm never certain what to think when I open up a book to begin reading. Sometimes I enter with great anticipation based on what I believe the book will be about, a predetermined interest in the subject matter, or the reputation of the author. Having never written a book before, I now realize that you may be thinking the same thing as you read this work, as well.

Some books I just can't put down, others are more difficult to read. I become deeply involved in some, while others find their way to the bottom of the stack fairly quickly. So here's the honest scoop, it may save you some time.

If you are looking for a treatise on the stages of grief or how to handle difficult times, you may be disappointed. If you are looking for wisdom from an inspiring personality or spiritual warrior who has faced life's darkest moments, and come through victorious, you *will* be disappointed. If you are looking for a self-help book that details how I "got over it," go ahead and place this one at the bottom of the pile. And forget knowing the author. Unless you go to my church, live in my small town, or have been a part of one of the few Churches I have served, you have probably never heard of me.

I guess that is the way I want this to be. You see, although this book tells Matt's story, and to a lesser degree mine, it is not about me—or Matt either for that matter. Matt was no doubt the greatest Christian I have ever met, but he was still not Christ.

This book is actually a bit selfish. I have written so I won't forget. You see, during the time frame this book covers, I came to know Christ and His love in new ways I could never fully express. I witnessed a love story that, if properly scripted, Hollywood studios would fight over. I lived in the arms of Jesus for more than a year directly beside someone who walked with Him much closer than I did. I know what it is like to depend on my relationship with Christ to find the courage just to get up and go to work.

And today I am desperately afraid I will somehow forget.

After ten years at a single job, it is possible for an employee to have ten years' experience. It is also equally possible that another employee working for the same time period may glean one year of experience ten times. Along the way I learned so many things that I don't want to forget. I also don't want to forget Matt. I just can't. I want to be the one that learned from all of it.

It seems somehow unfair to just "go on" and not remember that I shared life with my son for a precious few years. And therein lie the opposing forces that drive the long process of recovery—I want to forget, and I dare not forget. I want to forget so the pain will stop. I dare not forget for fear it was all in vain.

Many of the participants in this drama will remain unnamed. I have done this intentionally for several reasons. First, I want to protect their privacy. Also, I would never begin to think I could speak for my children, my wife or any of Matt's friends or relatives. Their journeys are not mine. They have learned other lessons and experienced their own pain.

Secondly, others who were a part of this journey made their sacrifices for us quietly, and I do not wish to cheapen those sacrifices in any way. Finally, so many gave so much that I fear I would leave someone out. I have mentioned a few by name. It is not that they are any better than anyone else; it's just that it seemed appropriate in context.

I am also quite aware that what I have written may never be widely read. But just in case it is, I want to be certain that readers understand exactly why I have written this book. So, if you haven't yet placed this book to the bottom of the pile, join me and help me remember this story that so profoundly changed our lives.

The lessons are not mine. I do not to claim to be an expert on grief. No—these lessons came from God. They are lessons that He taught *me*, a career vocational minister, through the loss of my son.

Thanks for reading as I share these lessons learned from a broken heart.

PART 1
Merry Christmas

CHAPTER 1

'Twas The Night Before Christmas...

#1

Matt is still in remission. He is grown and has four awesome boys. He and Lauren have been happily married for more than 10 years now. Matt is now successfully serving a Church as Youth Pastor. We win!

#2

Matt continued his battle with cancer for eight long months. We tried everything there was to try. Matt slipped into eternity where angels greeted him, and where his loved ones wait. We win!

#3

Matt is living with the disease, on borrowed time. Our lives are measured by a series of days; four, eleven, twenty-one... no longer weeks or months. But all that is ok, because we're still in the fight and that alone means we win!

Do you see it? There is only one thing in common with these three stories; we win. And to be quite honest, at the time of this writing, I don't know which it will be. You may be reading this not knowing how your journey will come out either. There is only one thing that will keep you in the race—whatever the outcome. Those who hope in Christ win.

It was Christmas Eve 2007 when I wrote those words. I was all alone in the public area of a hotel-like facility for family members overlooking the main entrance of a large hospital. It was anything but a "silent night." The battle raging deep in my soul robbed me of sleep, reason, and peace. I was in the middle of an epic wrestling match. I struggled with the reality that one of those three scenarios was most likely to be Matt's outcome.

And I had to be content with whichever one it was.

It was only one week earlier that the journey had begun. Matt, our 21-year old son, had only recently been troubled by a cough that just wouldn't quit. He also had a severe backache. Two weeks earlier, we had presented our Christmas musical at church. Matt, working as my music assistant, was responsible for returning the rented lighting equipment to Dallas.

Because we lived in a small East Texas town, any specialized equipment had to come from a larger city, this one some forty miles to the west. He was complaining of a backache even then. So I went into "dad mode." "Suck it up," I said. And Matt did. He loaded the van and set out to return what we had rented. It was no big deal for Matt. After all, it was for the church, and Matt loved our church.

Matt was nine years old when his mom, Shaunda, and I were married. I was already serving Family Fellowship of Greenville as music Pastor. I had been through a difficult divorce a few years earlier, and I was raising my two children—Joey, who was eleven then, and Lynmarie, who was thirteen—as a single dad.

Shaunda brought her "package deal" with her, and what a package it was. In addition to Matt, it included a daughter Jodi who was fifteen, and a son Brian who was seven. Before this great blessing in my life, I was doing my best to balance single parenting, work, little league baseball, girl's softball, and a rather awkward stint as a "cheerleader mom."

Shaunda and I met at a Texas-style rodeo sponsored by an adult class in our church. Only later would I discover that I had been "set up" by my Pastor and Shaunda's parents. By then, it really didn't matter—I had fallen hopelessly in love. When the time seemed right, we made the decision to blend our families.

When you do the math, it all made sense. Each child was two years apart. It was obviously the right thing to do, and we could pull it off without a hitch. Right? Well, perhaps not.

I am often asked about blending families. The only advice I give is to take a few nights and watch every episode of the Brady Bunch. For those who may be too young to remember, this was a popular 1970s TV show depicting the blending of a dad with three boys and a mom with three girls. When you're finished with the final episode, turn the TV off and take a moment or two to realize that blending a family will be *nothing at all* like what you have just watched. But that is subject matter for another book—one I most certainly will *not* attempt to write.

At the beginning of our relationship, there was a bit of discussion about what my role would be in the lives of Shaunda's children. I couldn't be "Dad," they already had a dad. I could be "stepdad," but the prefix can carry some negative connotations. It implies that a man has "stepped in" to fulfill the role in the absence of a real father. Shaunda's children had a dad. Eventually we just settled on the idea that I would be "another dad," and I was honored to be in that role.

Matt was a tremendous young athlete. I still have many of the home run balls to prove it. After one successful season of freshman high school football however, something deep inside inspired him to pursue music instead. So he did.

His love for music began years earlier when I gave him my old guitar, taking it from my closet and blowing the dust from its neglected strings. I gave him a quick lesson about how to form a few simple chords, and that was all it took to fan the flame.

Early on, Matt would retreat into his room for hours at a time. It took many weeks before the strange sounds emanating from behind his closed door even remotely sounded like music.

One night was especially memorable.

Have you ever listened to a pre-teen boy sing? It was hilarious. I could swear the cows in the field behind our house had gathered at the barbed wire fence to see if one of their loved-ones was in trouble. Shaunda and I were enjoying a quiet evening at home drinking sweet tea and watching made-for-TV movies, but it was hard to focus as Matt's "music" interrupted us relentlessly. It was the same four chords and the same lyric, over and over. At each commercial break, we walked down the hallway to his bedroom door to listen. We laughed a lot, only to hurry back to the living room for the next part of the movie.

On one of these trips down the hall, I noticed a slight, albeit very slight, rhythm developing—a strumming pattern. The vocal strains (and I do mean "strains") were growing stronger. The combination soon transcended the TV show. Matt was making real music.

At first, Shaunda and I chuckled. Don't misunderstand me please, we were proud of him, but it was also more than a little funny. Sometimes the chuckles turned into full laughter. But don't worry, Matt was never aware. He certainly couldn't hear us—he was making too much noise.

That night, he played the four chords used in the chorus of *HOW GREAT IS OUR GOD* over and over for hours. The lyrics were powerful:

How Great is our God,
Sing with me How Great is Our God.
All will see How Great,
How Great is our God.

The rhythm became steady, and the words resonated with us. Each time he sang that chorus, it came out a little louder and more confident.

On our final trip down the hallway that evening, our laughter turned to tears when we realized what was really happening. What had started as a single music lesson weeks earlier had crossed the indeterminable border from words and chords to an actual intimate experience with God. Matt had made his first transition from music to *worship*.

How could we ever have known that this one song would become the anthem of Matt's life—and later the soundtrack of his death?

CHAPTER 2

The Wake Up Call

During the next few years of Matt's high school career, he led worship in our small East Texas town at "The Attic," our teen church. Soon, he would carry his guitar into "big church," and lead worship right beside me each Sunday.

After graduation, he earned a full-ride scholarship in music from Jacksonville Baptist College, a small school a few hours from our home. This prevented him from every week involvement at our church, but it did lead to an Associate's degree.

"Congratulations," I joked with Matt as he neared the end of this phase of his college education, "but keep your day job. Very soon you'll be paying for the rest of college." However, an audition brought him yet another scholarship—this time to Criswell College in Dallas, where he planned to complete a Bachelor's degree in religious studies. This school was closer to home and allowed him to serve an internship in youth and music at our church, not to mention taking his place back on the platform right beside me again.

Final exams in December 2007 marked the half-way point in Matt's third year of Bible College. The promise of a career in ministry was very close. He was home for the holiday break and for our Christmas musical—*THERE IS PEACE IN THE WORLD TONIGHT.*

A week later, the son of a longtime friend was getting married. The son was a police officer in our town where I also served as police chaplain. He had asked me months earlier to perform the ceremony. I was thrilled and immediately said yes. Shaunda and I were at the rehearsal the night before.

After that Friday wedding rehearsal, I hit the streets to work wearing my police hat. I had been involved with local law enforcement as a chaplain ever since I first entered church ministry. That involvement continued wherever I served as a pastor. Eventually, I became a Texas Peace Officer and had a nineteen-year parallel career as a police officer. So, I worked early into the following Saturday morning as a Deputy Constable and Warrant Officer for Hunt County and looked forward to sleeping in that Saturday morning—December 22.

I vaguely remember Shaunda nudging me early that morning to tell me she was taking Matt to the hospital. He had been coughing and experiencing back pain for two weeks. Now, there was a new symptom—Matt was having trouble breathing. "OK," I responded, "Let me know what happens." I was barely awake. I rolled over and quickly went back to sleep. It was not my finest moment.

An hour later my phone rang. The next words I heard snapped me awake and alert. Shaunda said, "Get dressed, and get down here right away. Something's wrong, I can tell!"

I didn't bother with a shower, but was on the way to the hospital immediately. Because of my police work, I knew the code to the ambulance entrance, enabling me to bypass the public entrance, and the accompanying red tape. Thankfully, the emergency room wasn't busy that morning. I ignored protocol and walked directly into the small room reserved for doctors. I was relieved to see that the doctor in charge in the ER that morning was someone I knew and respected.

"Hey Joe, what are you doing here today?" he asked.

"You have my son here."

I saw his eyes drop down and to the right—and my heart dropped with them.

"Sit down," he said, as he pushed out a chair.

There was a lump in my throat, one that would remain for the next several years.

Doctor Pierce said, "There is a mass right here," as he pointed at the X-ray photo with the end of a black pen. It's funny how you remember the small things. "It's pretty large", he continued, "It has his heart and other internal organs displaced. That's why Matthew can't breathe very well."

Because of my police work, I have had some experience with trauma. There is a term used in law enforcement: "non-survivable injury." It is a term used when someone may be physically alive, but their injury appears to be so severe that without a direct intervention of God, they most likely won't survive.

Matt's issue was not a traumatic injury. Yet, one glance at the X-ray brought the term "non-survivable" to mind. The mass was so large I feared it would not allow his body to sustain life. At that moment, I knew in my heart that this "mass" would most likely take my son's life. I also knew that, for now, this was my private burden to bear.

"Go on in the room with your Family," Doc Pierce said. "I'll be there in a minute to talk to all of you."

It was only a dozen steps to that room. But with each step my feet seemed to gain an additional pound. I reached the room and stood outside the closed door, summoning every ounce of my wavering courage. I finally pushed it open.

"Hey guys," I said with as much sunshine as I could muster. I smiled and made brief eye contact with Shaunda. I immediately looked down and to the right, instantly realizing that I was doing exactly what Doctor Pierce had done when I first saw him.

After a few moments, Dr. Pierce entered the room and set into motion a series of events none of us could have ever imagined only ninety minutes earlier. There were ambulances, stat transfers, surgeons, doctors, nurses, oncologists, and a host of other peace-shattering things. All this time, my son was struggling to breathe, and it was getting worse. It was now nearly noon, two days before Christmas Eve.

It was our first brush with despair, but it would not be our last. Dr. Pierce made repeated visits. He was looking for a hospital and an oncologist who would be available to take Matt's case. But it seemed that every hospital in the area was unavailable and staffed with only skeleton crews because of the holidays.

Although we did not fully understand it at the time, we were learning that some forms of cancer could be aggressive beyond a person's wildest imagination. Bear in mind, Matt had only been "sick" for a couple of weeks.

As we waited in that small room, minutes seemed like hours, and the hours seemed like days. I learned a powerful lesson: *Time is relative to the event.* Even though I was a career Pastor, apparently I had much to learn. This was a wake up call to my spirit. Better listen to the Teacher.

Why do two minutes in a dentist's chair seem longer than two weeks on vacation? Why do two weeks on vacation seem so much shorter than two hours in a small hospital emergency room? Because, time is relative to the event.

As I pondered this, a familiar face appeared at the door. I recognized the uniform of our local emergency medical service personnel. I also recognized the smile of a man I had worked with many times before, sometimes beside the road at a tragic accident, and other times at the scenes of a horrific crime. I had repeatedly watched him work, and I knew he was good at his job. I had seen him perform complicated life saving techniques on more than one occasion. I knew that if *I* couldn't breathe, he was someone I would want there for me.

And I was thrilled he would be there for Matt.

He looked at Matt and said: "I'm your ride." He looked at me and said, "I'll take care of your son." I looked down—

and most likely to the right. I think I said "Thanks," but I'm not certain he could understand me. I fought to speak through the tears and that chronic lump in my throat.

I was learning another valuable lesson: *There are places that your kids have to go where you can't go with them.* When this happens, you are unspeakably grateful for anyone in whom you have confidence. You want to be certain they know exactly what to do. I would apply this same lesson again. I would soon learn that wherever this journey would take Matt, there would always be someone with him who already knew the way.

CHAPTER 3

Precious Cargo

The Mobile Intensive Care Unit (MICU) carrying my son departed for Presbyterian Hospital in Dallas. Dr. Pierce had found an oncologist who would treat Matt immediately, even on such short notice, and just two days before Christmas Eve.

Shaunda and I drove by our house, threw some clothes in a suitcase, and headed for Dallas. On the way, I remembered to call my friend's son to tell him I would not be able to perform his wedding ceremony. I had already called my brother-in-law (also a staff pastor at our church) to ask him to cover for me. Speaking of my brother-in-law, I have said many times that his actions in the months to follow would give all brothers-in-law a bad name. He was less like the stereotypical "brother-in-law," and so much more a great friend.

Upon arrival, we discovered that there was a hotel located *inside* the hospital. Since most hospitals pare down their patient count during the holidays, there were fewer family members on site, and we easily found a room. It was very nice, with a private bathroom. It provided a comfortable place of solitude.

That first day was pretty much a blur. We stayed with Matt until he told his mom she had to leave the room. She had planned to camp out beside his bed. He insisted otherwise. It would not be the last unselfish decision he would make. As a matter of fact, his life would become completely unselfish.

The next day was Sunday, December 23. I departed Dallas early that morning and made the 50-minute trip back to our church in Greenville. It would become a familiar trek. I arrived at church, led Worship, and then left immediately after the music in second service. I went by the house to collect some items we had forgotten in our haste the day before. While there, I grabbed a small artificial Christmas tree that adorned our mantle year after year. I also found a few strands of miniature Christmas lights and some presents—one for each of the kids.

I have always loved Christmas, perhaps because in many ways I have never grown much past twelve years old. Big and busy Christmases have always been great memories for me. Whether it was the family "Disney Christmas," including "mouse-like" gifts for each child—and a promised trip to Disney World for all—or the "Great Game Room Christmas." I loved them all.

As the kids grew up, they went their separate ways. Both Joey and Lynn spent their last high school year with their mom, when they were seventeen. The years and miles soon separated us. But we were separated in other ways, as well. Through the years I prayed for just one more Christmas together.

I arrived back at the hospital on Sunday afternoon, and much to Matt's dismay, I decorated his room. Nothing too fancy, mind you, but enough to get a few eye-rolls from him. At nightfall, Matt again sent his mom to our room and we all settled down.

The next day would be Christmas Eve.

Matt had been dating a wonderful young lady named Lauren. We had grown to love her very much, and we had enjoyed spending quite a bit of time with her and Matt. She joined us in the hotel suite and stayed by Matt's side every possible moment those first days. She would be with us—and Matt—for the duration.

Early the next morning we realized that Lauren had never returned to the hotel room. Shaunda said she was going back to Matt's room to check on them. "No," I insisted. Lauren was with him, and he'd rather have her there than us anyway. If she needed us, she would call. But Shaunda insisted, so I came up with a compromise: I would go.

I got dressed and began the fifteen-minute walk from the hotel room area to the oncology section of the hospital. As I neared Matt's room, I noticed the hallways were dark and his door was shut. I gently turned the door handle and quietly opened the door, expecting to find Matt asleep. After all, he had been given medication, and the continued oxygen flow assuaged his breathing difficulty, providing welcome relief.

I slowly slipped inside, actually quite proud of my police-like stealth. It took a few seconds for my eyes to adjust, but I could tell that Matt was indeed asleep. As a matter of fact, the only sound in the room was the oxygen coming from a port in the wall. I also noticed something else.

There was one of those not-very-comfortable, plastic hospital chairs pulled up next to the bed. Lauren was in it. She was bent a full ninety-degrees at the waist. And her neck was bent another ninety-degrees so that her cheek was flat on the hospital bed directly next to Matt. Her beautiful long black hair was draped beside her. She, too, was asleep.

I quietly slipped back out the door and wept all the way back to our hotel room. I was overwhelmed by what I had just seen. I knew at that moment that Matt was in great hands even when his mom or I were not in that room with him. There was no doubt in my heart that this young girl was filled with deep, unselfish, and sacrificial love for Matt.

The X-rays and MRIs from the day before indicated the need for emergency surgery. Just what that meant, no one seemed to know, or at least they were reluctant to speculate. "We won't know for sure until we get in there," was the consensus. "We've got to see what that mass is, where it is, and to what it may be attached." There was only one sure thing—it couldn't wait.

Not even for Christmas.

It didn't really feel much like Christmas Eve, at least at first. The fairly typical Texas morning was clear and crisp. Shaunda and I prayed together and then skipped breakfast. The walk back to Matt's room included several twists and turns. The facilities seemed to be in a perpetual state of renovation. When we arrived we got the pre-op "talk."

Then we went to the waiting room. They told us Matt would be in surgery for at least two to four hours.

As I left that small conference room to enter the general waiting room, I imagined what other families were doing on that Christmas Eve morning. I wondered what I would be doing if we were all simply at home where we belonged, wrapping the final gifts, and preparing things for Christmas dinner. My feet now seemed to weigh a hundred pounds each. I pushed open the door and found myself face to face with a Christmas miracle. It would not be the last I would experience that week either.

The large waiting room was completely full, and I recognized every face.

There were hugs, and smiles, and tears—lots of tears. Donuts, sausage rolls, and coffee appeared, courtesy of someone who would soon be known as our family angel. She became a regular visitor. And there were so many tears.

Did I mention the tears?

Every time I tried to sit down the door would open again, as more and more friends and family came in. We smiled, ate, and laughed. Another lesson from a broken heart became so clear to me: *The darkest journey is made a little easier with the help of fellow travelers.*

Then, the door opened again.

This time, my heart instantly became ice cold. It was the doctor. A hush fell over the room, and I glanced at my watch. Barely thirty minutes had passed—not the two to four hours we had expected. His words were grim: "too large," "too aggressive," "too entangled." What I really heard was, "no hope, no hope, no hope." This was the first time I identified the "up and down" aspects of this whole experience as the "roller coaster."

Once again the room filled with tears. No one knew what to say. No one knew what to do. Someone said that we should pray. I still don't remember who that was. We all stood and joined hands in one giant circle around the circumference of the room. It was very quiet, but for hushed whimpers and some ironically out-of-place festive holiday music in the background.

After a few moments of silence, I realized that no one was going to say a word. It was up to me to pray. No one else was going to start. I guess it was to be expected. After all, I *was* a pastor and police chaplain. I had been in these situations many times before. I knew exactly what to do and say. But the truth was, I had never been *here* before.

If ever a situation demanded the most eloquent prayer possible, this was it. There was so much at stake. This was my son. This was life and death. In that crucial prayer situation the only words running through my head were, "Please, God, no!"

Over and over.

There would be no eloquence on this day, at least not from me. I opened my mouth, and voiced one of the shortest prayers I have ever prayed. It was all I had. Perhaps not verbatim, but here is the sense of what I said:

"God, nothing that has happened in the past three days has surprised You, and You also know how this is all going to turn out. The only question is: do we trust You or not?"

There it was, laid out for all to see. No form, no structure. No intercession, no supplication, and certainly no eloquence. Yet, herein lies perhaps the greatest lesson for this broken heart to learn: ***Our Sovereign God sometimes chooses paths for us that may hold pain, disappointment, and loss.***

In fact, God even laid out such a plan for His very own Son. The question should never be, "Will God come through for us?"' or "Will He bring this matter to a conclusion that pleases me?" The path was already laid for us to follow. The better question is, "Do I trust Him or don't I?" I was powerless to alter the outcome of Matt's medical condition. It remained to be seen, however, what the journey would do to me.

The remainder of the day was a blur. I recall many phone calls and the visits of several friends and family members. I also remember the many apologies when people had to leave to attend family functions. I learned here another great lesson. I could tell in people's eyes that in spite of the despair and darkness that began to envelop our lives: *there are those who will choose to take the journey with us at great cost to themselves.*

I now know what it means to be surrounded by circumstances that make you feel as if you may slip under the crashing waves at any moment. I also know what it means to have others who will come along side you, take you by the hand, and keep you from drowning. And I know what it means to appreciate them in ways deeper than I ever imagined.

That was when I wrote the words I shared at the beginning of this book.

Later, everyone went home. After all, it was Christmas Eve. Shaunda was in our room, and I was all alone in the public area of that hotel, staring through a huge window overlooking the hospital's main entrance. And another lesson gripped my heart: *there is a part of every journey that has to be experienced alone.*

It's the part of the journey that comes down to you and God. I'm sure God makes certain that this takes place. It's a place with no pretense and no bravado—only brutal honesty. I had to take this journey, and it had to be taken alone.

There would also be a part of the journey yet to come that Matt would have to take alone.

Only later would I realize that I was *never* alone—nor was Matt.

CHAPTER 4

Merry Christmas

Because of what was happening, Christmas in 2007 should have been the worst any of us had ever experienced. We faced the incredible shock of the sudden and unexpected onslaught of a serious illness on a seemingly healthy young man. Not only that, but during his morning rounds the doctor had actually used one of the most dreaded words in the English language for the first time. The "C" word—*cancer.* He couldn't say for sure what kind, and he wouldn't even venture a guess at a prognosis. He did, however, tell us that additional surgery was not an option.

Matt started chemotherapy on Christmas Day.

As I write this section, I am sitting in the beautiful lobby of our church. And I am again reminded of the numerous times God's grace has rushed to the surface. At times the whole thing seemed surreal. But there was a hospital bed two days before Christmas. There was a doctor who would give up his Christmas Eve to help Matt. There was another doctor who would give up his Christmas Eve to plan treatment. There were nurses who gave up holiday time with their families to work around the clock.

Keep in mind the urgency of this matter. This disease was so aggressive that Matt went from "my back hurts" to barely being able to breathe in only two weeks. Who knows what might have happened had we waited a couple more days before taking him to the hospital?

Through it all, what was perhaps the greatest miracle of all was beginning to dawn on us.

Matt did not complain.

Let me say that again, because you may consider it hyperbole. Matt *never* complained. Not once. I complained, but not he. I experienced debilitating panic and despair, but Matt didn't. I felt the insufferable darkness fueled by anger. I wept and cried until I had no more tears. But not Matt.

He never blamed God.

That Christmas morning, the three of us exchanged simple gifts and did the best that we could to tap into the holiday spirit. Lauren finished her family's Christmas celebration and found her way back to Matt's bedside early that morning. As a matter of fact, Lauren, herself just a young lady, displayed a commitment to God and Matt that defied description.

At one point late in the journey Shaunda and I agreed that we were sharing front row seats to a love story that Hollywood would never be able to comprehend, let alone portray. Through this "picture" I learned another lesson: *honest and unselfish love gives even when there is little hope of return.*

After a while, Shaunda's sister, Deidre, and her husband, Steve, arrived. Then, Jodi and Brian came by, as well as Joey and Lynn. And there it was—the Christmas I had wanted for so many years. Right there in that hospital room, with just that tiny tree, a couple strands of lights, and some simple gifts, we celebrated Christmas.

Matt had given me one of the greatest Christmas gifts I had ever received. I had even prayed for it so many times. It was the Christmas gift I had desired more than anything else. We were all together. All of us.

It felt so good I almost felt *bad.*

That Christmas was storybook material. It became such a precious family holiday for our family and extended family. I had already prepared Shaunda. We had so many visitors on Christmas Eve that I didn't want her to believe it was always going to be like this. We eventually learned that "lots of visitors" may not always be what you may want, but for us, it was nothing short of a lifeline. I suggested to her, because it was Christmas, people were busy with their own families and might not have a lot of time for us on this day.

I was so very wrong.

Long before lunchtime, they came—family and friends, police officers, and politicians, but mostly people from our wonderful church. I have served on staff at several churches over the past thirty years. It has not always been easy. There have been personality conflicts, pressure-packed moments, and long hours. And the pay wasn't always all that great. As a pastor and law enforcement chaplain, I have poured my life into people.

Don't misunderstand me, I always felt blessed to be the "giver" and not the "taker." This always made me feel good about who I was and made me feel as if I were truly a *minister*. But for this phase of the journey, it would be different. We were in a church we loved, one that loved us. And just to state the obvious—we were very needy.

What started as a trickle soon became a downpour. By nightfall, literally hundreds of people had come through the door. They brought food, cards, and gifts—but more importantly, they brought love and hope. Some came and left, while others came and *stayed*. Some offered words of encouragement. Some said nothing at all. Some I called by name, others I met for the first time.

Early on, nurses and doctors came into the waiting room to ensure we were behaving and not causing damage to the facility. Later, hospital personnel came from throughout the hospital just to watch. They were seeing Jesus in the lives of people, whether they realized it or not.

At one point, we learned that a family in our church worked at the hospital. They gave "free parking" coupons and helped us with reduced lodging rates. I don't know what they actually said or did, but shortly after they left, the highest ranking hospital administrator on duty came by with yet another handful of parking coupons, information about free rooms, and the generous offer to be of any help needed. I still may have some of those parking coupons in today.

Throughout Christmas day and well into the evening, we laughed, wept, and prayed. It was a scene that looped again and again. The small tables in the waiting room were regularly cleared and replenished with food and drinks. I can't even venture a guess as to how many people ate Christmas dinner with our family that year, but I know it was well into the hundreds. At times, the gathering would shrink to only twenty or thirty, but most of the time it stayed steady at seventy or eighty.

And this was *Christmas.*

Everyone who came to minister to our family had sacrificed precious family time. Whether they realized it or not, those sacrifices would remain in our hearts throughout our journey. As a matter of fact, they still give me a sense of balance and buoyancy today. With or without words, the messages were clear and forthright.

We were not going to be alone.

At one point in the afternoon, Matt's nurse came in with an IV pump and bag. He was getting his first dose of chemo for Christmas.

Later that night, it was time to leave and return to our room. Shaunda wanted to stay the night with Matt, but yet again he wouldn't go for it. I leaned over and kissed my son on the forehead. Matt and I had developed a unique ability to communicate through the years, often without ever saying a word. Maybe it was musical—the hours in rehearsal listening to the nuance of each other's performance and intricate rhythms. Perhaps it was the hours spent riding around in my patrol car. Or maybe it was all the time we sat in my church office discussing life in the ministry. However it happened, we had a kind of same-wavelength connection. I was very grateful for it. Somehow, some way, Matt had morphed from being my son to being my friend.

After I gently kissed Matt's forehead, I whispered in his ear. "Thanks Matt, for the greatest Christmas gift a Dad could ever have." He smiled and said, "You're welcome." We both knew exactly what I meant.

All the kids were together for Christmas.

Shaunda and I returned to our hotel room, changed clothes, switched off the light, and literally fell into bed exhausted. What should by all rights have been a tragedy, was instead a *triumph*.

A few times that night, I woke up briefly and looked around the room to see if Jesus himself might be there with me. I know that may sound strange to some, but it's just that his presence was so real. He was so close.

I never want to forget that.

PART 2

Happy Holidays

CHAPTER 5

The Long Road Ahead

Much of the journey from that *first* Christmas to the next one remains a bit undefined in my memory. Here, however, is a barometer of sorts. Every major holiday in between those two Christmases was spent with Matt as a patient in one form or another. The interim involved a series of lengthy visits to clinics and doctor's offices. What I do remember vividly, however, is the tears—so many tears.

But also some laughter.

That first Christmas, I remember Matt asking a visitor what he had gotten for Christmas. I'm not sure what the young man's exact reply was—something about a new game system perhaps. But I well remember Matt's response. "Wow, that's cool. Know what I got? I got a tumor!"

I remember Matt telling another person that he was not really "sick," he "just had cancer." To another he said, "The rumors of my illness are greatly exaggerated. I just have a headache, and I'm due to go home at any moment." Each time he laughed. Then we laughed.

Then we cried.

Along the way, I began, at least in an imaginative way, to put those tears in a small "bottle." I kept it with me. There was never a clue when I might need it again.

It quickly became obvious to even casual observers that Matt was having a significant impact on everybody around him. That first week I watched Matt leave his hospital room, his bed guided by a rather large young man on the hospital staff. They were on their way to yet another series of tests. As they rolled out of the room, Matt was already joking with him.

The two of them returned about an hour later still laughing and smiling. The young man stepped on the locking mechanism to secure the bed in place, then he gave Matt a high-five. Turning to leave, the young staffer suddenly spun back around and abruptly asked, "Why are you smiling, don't you know you have cancer?"

Matt replied, "You'd smile too if you had Jesus in your heart."

I don't remember that hospital employee's name, and he probably doesn't remember mine. But I'm confident he's never forgotten Matt's. This was another one of those crazy things that fueled my internal conflict. I was devastated by the events of the past few weeks, but I was so proud of my son that I could barely speak.

Matt was released from his initial hospitalization after only ten days. Further rounds of Chemo were scheduled—seven days of Chemo every twenty-one days. All of it at the hospital. Life had changed so drastically in less than two weeks.

And yet the journey had only just begun.

CHAPTER 6

The First "R"

Matt's cancer had manifested faster than any case I had ever heard about. He was fine, then his back hurt, then his chest hurt, and then he couldn't breathe. Just like that. And the vicious cycle took just two weeks to reach critical mass. I asked myself several times, "What just happened?" Why had our world suddenly come to a standstill? How could the wheels come off so quickly?

As swiftly as the cancer grew, choking the very life out of my son, the chemo beat it into submission. I had never seen anything like it. My mother died of cancer. And as a minister, I have been with more families than I can count who have battled this unseen and merciless enemy. It is usually a painstakingly slow process. But not in Matt's case.

When Matt entered the emergency room in Greenville on December 22 because of his inability to breathe, he was given oxygen. Tests confirmed that he was unable to get oxygen into his bloodstream. The clear tube in his nose became a part of his body for the next few days. Within thirty-six hours of when he started chemotherapy Christmas day, the tube came out. Matt's blood oxygen levels were up, and he could once again breathe without difficulty.

Before being released from the hospital, the seemingly endless rounds of tests identified the type of cancer, then the subtype, and on and on. Matt's diagnosis was a rare form of non-Hodgkin's lymphoma—a type typically seen in older males. The doctors told us the good and bad of it. The bad news was that this was a cancer described as highly-aggressive (we already knew that part). The good news was that it was a cancer that responded well to chemotherapy.

They were right on both counts.

Soon Matt was feeling much better, and he resumed his normal life. He went back to work, leading worship at Family Fellowship Church, as well as serving in the church's middle school ministry. Other than becoming tired easily, he seemed to be relatively normal. His hair did not fall out—at least at first—his color was good, his back did not hurt any longer, and best of all, he could easily breathe.

The "down the road" view was still a bit scary, but the turbulent storm that had arisen without warning—and so quickly—was now completely off our radar. Had we just dreamed this? Could the doctors be wrong? Had God allowed these events merely to test Matt? Or was it to create a platform for a miracle for all to see? All that had transpired the previous three weeks (yes, just three weeks) was surreal.

The remaining six weeks of Matt's first round of chemo began to appear, well, unnecessary. He seemed fine. But we were assured that the reason for the treatments was to hit the cancer harder than it had hit Matt. Aggressive treatment would bury this evil marauder in a deep grave. We were beginning to feel like we had "dodged a bullet." My spirits began to lift and I felt like setting them free to soar to the heavens.

Then I would remember the X-ray I had seen that first morning.

When it was time for Matt's six-week checkup, they repeated the blood work and diagnostic tests from his hospital stay. We only knew these tests by a series of three letters—letters that have become words in our vocabulary. Like CAT and PET. These tests were a yardstick, so we could measure success—and see ultimate victory. The morning of the check-up, Shaunda, Matt, Uncle Steve, and I drove to Dallas early.

I have a great job.

Did that last sentence seem a bit out of place to you? Let me explain. I was able to take time off from work to go with Matt to the doctor. That was a great privilege, one I would enjoy more times than really I wanted to in the months to come. I worked at a church where I was loved and supported. I worked with a group of people who blessed me throughout the journey.

I was with Matt that morning for the tests and the follow-up visit with the doctors. We waited a couple of hours after the testing to be called back to meet the doctor in his office. It seemed like two *years*.

Matt's doctor was rather young, or at least he appeared to be. Matt's older siblings were about the doctor's age. Okay, I'll just say it—I was old enough to be his father. He was sharp, knowledgeable, and very kind. He brought in an extra chair since there were three of us, Matt, Uncle Steve, and me. Shaunda had chosen to remain in the waiting room. We anxiously watched as he moved to the glass panels that illuminated the test results from all those "three letter" tests and switched on the light.

On the left side was the "before"—the results from six-weeks earlier. That horrified Steve. I, on the other hand, had seen it before. It appeared as an ugly, white, and poorly defined mass of huge proportion when compared to the surrounding organs. It was frightening and disturbing—no question about it. It sent shivers of fear that were like a knife cutting my very soul.

Then he put up the "after" picture.

The mass was gone—c*ompletely.*

It was as if I could feel the warm summer breeze on my face at Six Flags in nearby Arlington Texas. I could hear the clanking of the gears on its rickety Texas Giant rollercoaster as it neared the top. The car slowed and then nearly stopped. We had climbed the first hill.

Excitement was welling up in my chest. I thought it might burst. Instead it was my eyes. It was like I was raising my hands high in the air as the rollercoaster car slipped over the top of that first hill and began to accelerate. I wanted to scream at the top of my lungs. I didn't care who heard me, or who thought I had lost my mind. Down the steep hill we went at breakneck speed.

I LOVE a rollercoaster!

There it was, the first "R"—**REMISSION.**

But the doctor—clearly wise beyond his years— cautioned us. This was indeed a great and unexpected victory, unlike "any he had ever seen." But it was still very early in the journey. There was still much to do and many more battles to fight. We soon needed to be sent to a new doctor—for a stem cell transplant.

But in that moment, all I felt was the wind in my face and the summer sun beating down on my forehead. And it dawned on me—it was the first time in weeks I had really breathed, as well.

CHAPTER 7

A Powerful New Drug

The next few months brought repeated periods of hospitalization for more chemotherapy. Matt's hair eventually fell out, but many of his friends, some church staff members, and even Uncle Steve, and Matt's pastor showed up with their hair missing as well to identify with him.

Matt now had a new primary oncologist, this one was a bone marrow transplant specialist. All of these changes brought new terminology and a new regimen of chemo, representing a totally different philosophy of treatment.

Matt's new specialist and his primary nurse would have a tremendous impact on our family during the weeks to come.

This new philosophy of treatment emphasized outpatient care as opposed to traditional time in the hospital. The distance from our home to the treatment center was exactly 49 miles, according to Mapquest. This was important because the distance at which Matt's insurance would cover lodging was 50 miles. We became acquainted with what we would affectionately refer to as "the apartment."

Actually, it was an apartment complex, a group of several buildings and part of a much larger complex that the medical center had purchased to use for their philosophy of outpatient treatment. We stayed in different apartments at different times, but always referred to them in the singular. Staying in the apartment kept Matt close enough to the hospital that kept his medical history, and yet far enough away to feel at least a little less sick. The setup seemed to work for Matt, which made it work for all of us. In between treatments, Matt and Shaunda would come home.

Since chemotherapy plays havoc with blood counts and the immune system, moving to the apartment and then back home was accompanied by some extraordinary cleaning rituals. In a word: Bleach. I got used to the smell of the stuff, and needless to say, our house was very clean.

This worked for me. I have been described as being a little "OCD" about more than a few things. I remember getting my seventh grade yearbook signed by a friend whose inscription read: *"To Joe Knight: A really cool kid whose favorite word is unsanitary."*

I have to admit, I laughed about that yearbook memory many times during all the cleanings and re-cleanings. Maybe my childhood friend was on to something. I still love the smell of bleach.

Throughout the following year, it became almost humorous when we were asked: "Who's staying at the apartment tonight?" Sometimes it was just Matt and Shaunda. It seemed like Lauren was always on the couch. Sometimes I was there. Sometimes it was Shaunda's parents who were there. Sometimes it was Matt's natural father and his new wife. Sometimes it was Shaunda's mom. Other times it was an eclectic group from all the above. But it was all good, and all for Matt, although sometimes he still just wanted us all to go home.

The Greenville Policed Department Officers Association sponsored a citywide blood drive and donor search as transplant day approached. This effort was led by one of the dearest friends I have ever had. There were advertising posters and there was coverage in the local newspaper. The efforts were promoted by radio stations and on the Internet. The call went out from briefing rooms to church platforms.

On the day of the blood drive, hundreds of people showed up. Some waited in line for hours—people from our church and other churches, police officers, fire fighters, lawyers, students, workmen, housewives, retirees, young people, older people, judges, and politicians. Once again, some were people we had known for years, others we barely knew, and many we had never met. At times, it seemed like a big family reunion or even a huge party.

One by one, they rolled up their sleeves and gave their blood. Many offered themselves as possible transplant donors. Matt and I spent a great part of the day walking around saying "thank you" over and over.

Transplant time arrived that May. Once again, a small crowd gathered at the hospital. The transplant team informed Matt that this was his second "birthday." He immediately responded that it was actually his third. He'd already had his second birthday when he trusted Christ as his Savior. Moved by his faith, few left Matt's presence that day with dry eyes, or without feeling they had been in the presence of a very special human being. I was yet again immensely proud.

And I added more tears to that bottle.

It was in Matt's nature to be a "stay at home" kind of guy. There was very little he couldn't handle as long as he had a soft drink to hold in one hand, and a television remote in the other. That way he could watch multiple ballgames at once. He also had a bit of the grandiose in him. And because Matt was tethered to the apartment by low blood counts, I was asked to play a small role in this "grandiose" side. Matt sent everyone—except me—out of the small holding room just before the transplant. It was my responsibility to hide the family video camera in a place where it would not be seen, and then turn on the recording mechanism. I was then instructed to leave and send Lauren in—alone. What happened next I only know because Matt let me watch the video.

It was something like "I can't get on one knee, because all these contraptions won't let me. But since this is my new 'birthday' I want you to know that I don't want to spend a moment of my new life without you. Will you marry me?"

Lauren said "Yes!"

A quick explanation of *why* she said yes might be in order. Yet I don't think I really understand why she did. By all common sense she should have run away. Had Lauren said "no" that day, who knows how much pain she might have saved herself? I had prepared Shaunda for that possibility. Honestly, had I been Lauren's dad that is exactly the advice I would have given her. As Matt's dad I could only sit back and be humbled by the fact that anyone could love my son that much.

Prayers all shared, and hugs all given, Matt was then off to the transplant room. No matching donor ever located, his own stem cells had been harvested earlier and were used in the procedure. It went off without a hitch.

The winter days had long since surrendered to spring, and now turned to summer. Matt was back at work and once again regularly leading worship on the platform at church right beside me—where he belonged.

During this part of the journey I learned the names of many powerful drugs, none of which I had heard before. They were the latest in the line of chemotherapy drugs— standard and experimental, as well as the latest and greatest cutting edge antibiotics. Injections seemed to work like magic, as Matt's blood counts came roaring back.

There were also some painkillers—potent narcotic concoctions to ease his suffering, if only for a little while. Of course, these came with words of caution about the risk of dependency from repeated use. If he became dependent, the withdrawal symptoms could be severe.

One drug, however, was far more powerful than any of the others. We discovered that it too provided relief and proved highly addictive. Withdrawal from this drug could also be painful. Yet all of us partook deeply from this drug. Without it we would have known only despair.

That powerful "drug" made us feel like a day at the amusement park riding that rickety rollercoaster with the cool breeze on our faces.

That drug was *HOPE.*

CHAPTER 8

The First Time through the Cornfield

It has been said that taking a new journey in life is similar to walking through a cornfield for the first time. The first time through, you trample down the corn stalks to make a path. If you ever go through that cornfield again, you tend to go the same way, since the path is clear.

I have come to realize that the direction of our lives is determined by a few major decisions. I have also learned that they are not what we expect them to be, They come without warning. And sometimes they pass us by, and we never notice they were there in the first place.

I have lived a blessed life. God has been more gracious to me than I deserve. When I was a very young boy, growing up in Akron, Ohio, I fell in love with the piano. My father promised to give me a new piano if I studied hard. I did, and he presented me with a black monstrosity that only vaguely resembled a piano. Fifty years later, I *still* remember how awful it smelled—like it had been in someone's basement for years. It couldn't even be properly tuned. But my folks were poor and it was free. They loved me and wanted me to have a piano—or at least something like a piano.

After a few years of lessons and practice I landed a job as a regular church pianist. I was eleven. When I was fifteen, I began studying piano with a private instructor at the University of Akron. I took my first worship leading job that same year. We were called "song-leaders" in those days. Oh, and I started a southern gospel quartet back then, as well.

Less than a year later, that quartet won a local talent contest, yielding my first recording. By the time I was 18, we had a 35-foot diesel bus and were travelling full-time in the summer and weekends all year long. I had also answered a call to full-time service and begun Bible college. My parents must have been insane—I would never have turned my kids loose with a road bus at that age.

During those "chasing the dream" years in the mid-70s, I literally walked music row in Nashville "peddling my wares." I also spent a night in Johnny Cash's house, and Bill Gaither bought my lunch. True stories. Both of those men knew they had helped me. I have told the stories over the years, they've been good for a few laughs. Eventually, however, I walked into the right office, and I found someone willing to take a chance on our young group.

Over the next few years, we performed at several large concert venues, many great Churches, and a few television shows. I had one original song published, released five recording projects, graduated from the Massillon Baptist College, got ordained, drove the wheels off our bus, barely missed a major label recording contract (a story that still brings tears to my eyes), and eventually went broke.

During those years I also successfully botched a relatively easy audition with the Cathedral Quartet. Years later, the late Glen Payne, their lead singer, would try to get me to laugh about my failed tryout. But it took me a long time to see the humor.

After five exciting years, I was 23 years old, and I was realizing that the road was not a good place to raise a family. I decided it was time to settle down. I took a position as Director of Special Music in my home church—a large congregation in Akron. Also around this time, I made my first solo recording, one that brought me an appearance at the 1984 World's Fair in Knoxville, an appearance on national television—and a wife.

I was married at the age of 24.

Over the next few years, I served two smaller churches, and I had my first involvement with law enforcement as a chaplain. Eventually, I took a job at another large church—this one in Springfield, Missouri. I had several great years there—and a few difficult ones, as well.

I led a large choir and a full orchestra in the church services, which were broadcast on local television. There were also major Christmas productions that drew people from across the region. I also used my time in Springfield to work on another Bachelor's degree, as well as a Master's. And I even led the church youth group for a couple of years. That part contributed to some of those "difficult" days I mentioned.

In addition to working at the Church, I developed a small business, writing and producing music for advertising, things like "jingles" and corporate videos. I had contracts with companies such as *Tyson Foods*, *Hammons Hotels*, and *General Foods*. I also produced custom recording sessions.

I played on a Branson gospel show, and later produced it for two seasons. I met Governor John Ashcroft and later was a guest in his home, as well as his parents' home. A singer/songwriter as well as a successful politico, I played on a recording session for him.

And I released a few more solo projects.

While in Springfield, my family and I bought an eight-acre gentlemen's farm, with plans of purchasing the adjoining eighty acres. Four of the eight acres included dense trees and a lake—all nestled in the beautiful Ozark Mountains. The other four acres featured two barns, an in-ground swimming pool, a new house, three cows, one sheep, one dog, four cats, and a pig. All of the animals did pretty well except the cats. I never figured out what happened to them. I actually considered writing a book way back then. I wanted to title it, "*I Am Too a Farmer: This Ain't Chocolate on My Tennis Shoes!*"

Thursday was "family night"—which meant a trip to the Mongolian BBQ. Friday was my day off, so it was "date day." I picked the kids up from school for some quality time with dad. We went to parks, played games, enjoyed "Max Movie Theatre," and "Game Nights." We played baseball, basketball, and softball. The activities changed through the years as the kids grew older—but not the time slot.

Friday *night* was set aside for mom and dad.

Sundays were all about church and then "show day" in Branson. Many weeks I would take one child with me to the theatre. I enjoyed one on one time, which always included a trip to the bulk-candy store located in the front of the venue.

I also served as a police chaplain, later becoming the vice president of that Springfield Missouri community organization. I was 37 years old and well blessed.

Then it all came crashing down.

My wife left. It was over. You can't be a Pastor and experience that kind of problem—not in Springfield, anyway. I was likely to lose my job, my house, my car, and maybe even my *kids*.

All of a sudden, it was just me and the kids at the house. That beautiful Ozark mountain home and the nice car in the driveway became financial leeches, sucking what little hope I had left from my very soul.

This couldn't be happening. I had lived a blessed life. I was raised by godly parents. I surrendered to the ministry at a young age. I had received Christ even earlier. I have often said, tongue-in-cheek, that I had chased wild women and done every kind of drug. I was an alcoholic and rode with a violent motorcycle gang until I was gloriously saved at the age of *seven*.

Yet here I was, for the first time in my life, at the beginning of a journey I did not want to take—at the edge of a cornfield. The outward journey would change me, inwardly—forever. It would also change how I thought about God.

I remember one Ozark autumn night, in particular. I had been wrestling with God for hours. How could He do this to me? After all, I was a good husband and good provider for my family. I was a minister, investing in people's lives. How could God be so uncaring? So far off? I had His "back" all through those years, why didn't He have *mine*?

As that sleepless night gave way to the early morning hours, I didn't want my children to hear the bitter outburst welling in my soul. As the Sun rose over the Ozark Mountains I ran out the back door into the empty pasture behind the house. I raised my hands to the sky and screamed at the top of my lungs: "God, do You have any idea what is going on here?" At first, there was only silence.

Then I heard the voice of God.

No, it wasn't audible. Morgan Freeman's voice didn't come booming from the heavens. It was, however, an authentic encounter with God like nothing I had ever experienced.

I was raised by God-fearing parents. My mother had often warned me about what God would do to anyone who challenged or disrespected Him. And I had done just that—in a huge way.

After a few moments of silence, I looked up, certain that the brightness of the freshly rising sun would soon be obscured by a small cloud. And that cloud likely contained a lightning bolt already aimed at my head. But there was no bolt from the blue, just words of assurance.

"My child, I am big enough for your questions."

That morning my heart was overwhelmed by God's great grace—and it remains so to this day. How could a God love me so much? How could He still love me after what I had felt in my heart? I began to weep and fell to my knees on the cold Missouri soil. I had so much to say, but all that came out was, "I'm sorry. I'm sorry."

The incredible grace of God had once again melted my bitter heart.

God knew exactly what was going on. Despite every circumstance, not to mention my bitter outburst, His status as God was not in the least threatened by me. He loved me. And a God who loved like that could most certainly be *trusted*.

After a few minutes of good heart cleansing, I went back inside the house, closing the door behind me. I walked upstairs where my children were, thankfully, still asleep. As I stood by my son's bed, I looked back over my shoulder. I could see the cornfield behind me, with a solitary path weaving through the middle.

In that path I had found strength. And what a lesson. *God is big enough for my questions.*

I could make it through. I really *could* do something with Christ that I could never do by myself.

When God takes the best...
I'll give Him Glory.
When my world comes crashing down,
I'll lift Him up
When we're faced with true reality,
We find our deepest need.
Our loving Lord designs the path,
It's not just random chance.
There is a purpose for the pain,
In every circumstance.
And when God takes the best,
You know He always has a reason.
When God takes the best...
I'll give Him praise.

CHAPTER 9
The Second "R"

The Fourth of July dawned typically Texas hot and humid. Shaunda, Matt, and I were on our way to Shaunda's family's with Mimi and Baddy. I once described a visit to their home as a kind of *Norman Rockwell* experience.

Think of a painting containing characters seated in bright wooden rocking chairs on a quaint front porch. The folks are sipping sweet tea and gazing at a radiant Texas sunset. Once Mimi and Baddy move into your heart, moving them out is next to impossible. Oh, and you must keep an up-to-date Texas dictionary nearby. It is absolutely essential when conversing with them.

The celebration would be another annual blend of people, barbecue, beans, fireworks, fishing poles, smoked cabbage, and potato guns. Always great fun. It would also be a very special time, for obvious reasons. A few months earlier, Matt had been at death's door, struggling for every breath. Our lives had been put on hold, and we were filled with uncertainty.

Now, we were filled with hope.

It was the first holiday of the year that Matt was not in the hospital. And with the successful stem-cell transplant behind him, he was back at work and planning his return to school that Fall. In fact, we all were finally back on track.

As evening approached, we were preparing to return to Greenville to catch the fireworks—a family tradition. Then, in a moment, four ominous words turned everything upside down, once again.

"Mom, my back hurts."

How quickly his cancer had manifested was still fresh in our minds, and we were afraid. The very next day, Matt started chemo again, and we were back on that rickety rollercoaster trying to climb yet another hill. We had been introduced to the second "R."

RELAPSE.

Matt now received another new type of chemotherapy and this caused his blood counts to fluctuate dramatically, particularly those that involve a person's ability to provide clotting. When blood does not properly clot, the body has a hard time stopping the bleeding even from a tiny cut.

We were back at home one hot summer night, when Matt developed a nosebleed. We had dealt with hard-to-stop bleeding before, but this was different. I will spare you the graphic details. But suffice it to say—there was a lot of blood. And it would not stop.

He was losing so much blood I was afraid to risk the drive all the way to Dallas. Instead, I grabbed a handful of bath towels, and we headed for the emergency room at our Greenville Texas hospital. We had not been back there since Christmas.

I still remembered the code to the back doors. We would have made a big mess, not to mention commotion and alarm, using the front entrance. But slipping in the back way and trying to remain calm could not prevent the triggering of a trauma code once the staff saw Matt.

They directed us to Trauma Room One. I had been in that same room many times over the years, as a chaplain or police officer. It is typically used for the serious illness or traumatic injuries. I had comforted and encouraged so many families in that room.

Now I was there with *my* family.

I knew most of the people on duty that night, as did Matt. He had gone to high school with the young lady serving as his primary nurse. Those on duty moved in and out of the room, never staying long. There was little they could do while waiting on an order of platelets from Dallas so they could jump-start the clotting process.

Meanwhile, they kept cleaning up the blood.

Again, I don't want to be graphic, but blood has a very distinctive *odor*. You don't notice it when there is just a little, but when there is a lot of blood you can't escape it. Having been to the location of so many accidents and crime scenes through the years, I have become somewhat conditioned. It was disconcerting, for sure, but it had ceased really bothering me long ago.

That night, however, I was very bothered. I had seen large amounts of blood in that very room before, but this was different. I found myself wondering why. I was tired, so it took me a while to understand.

It bothered me because it was my son's blood.

I knew that if it kept leaving his body and continued forming puddles on the floor, there would not be enough left to keep him alive.

There is a scripture verse that may be familiar to you. I have usually focused on the last half of the verse—the part about me.

> *...everyone who believes in him will not perish but have eternal life.*

However, that night in Trauma Room One, I was drawn to the first part:

> *For God loved the world so much that he gave...*

I prayed for the speedy arrival of the vehicle carrying what Matt needed. I prayed that the problem would get fixed before it was too late. I could not look the other way and allow my son to bleed to death.

In that moment, unlike any before or since, the sacrifice that God the Father made when He gave up His only Son was almost tangible. The Father had looked down from heaven on the day of His Son's crucifixion and watched that precious blood pool at the foot of the cross.

You see, God understands my pain because He too lost a Son. *These lessons He is teaching me come straight from His broken heart.* A heart broken by the sins of the world that would require the sacrifice of His only Son.

And when He could look no longer, He looked away. God made that choice freely, and Christ freely submitted to His Father's will.

Could I have done the same?

CHAPTER 10

Back Through the Cornfield

I remember reading Dr. Seuss books to our children. One of my favorites is the story of a large elephant named Horton. He had some very small friends. Horton called them the *Who*, and they lived in an town called Whoville.

No one could see the residents of Whoville—that is, no one except Horton. He loved these little people and felt responsible for their safety. The *Who* folks couldn't really understand Horton, and they sometimes questioned his honesty and sanity.

I have never been to Whoville and I have never seen a *Who*. However, I have been to *Why*ville. It is also intangible, yet quite real. I freely acknowledge that over the past few years I've spent a lot of time there.

So many times I've asked, *WHY*?

Again, I'd love to be able to say that I am a super-mature believer in Jesus and have never struggled with the "why" of Matt's illness. But that would not be honest. People who know me well would see right through such pretense. Yes, I struggled.

I still do.

Through my work with law enforcement over the past 30-plus years, I have met my share of victims—and suspects. I have also, on occasion, seen victims and suspects change places.

I have witnessed the hopelessness of wasted young lives more times than I care to remember. I have seen the bitter fruit of rebellious living with its boast, "I can do what I want, when I want to whomever I want." Absent an intervention of God's mercy, this decision making process eventually leads to self-destruction. I have found people lying in pools of vomit oblivious to their surroundings because of drug or alcohol abuse—or both. It's always a by-product of the unbridled power of choice. And sometimes they are lying in pools of blood, never to make choices again. Ever.

We are approaching the city limits and see the sign that says, Welcome to *Whyville*."

Why Matt? Now, Matt was a common sinner saved by grace, and he often seized the opportunity to prove it. Yet his life was ultimately defined by a series of good choices—the right ones.

When it came down to choosing between church youth camp and *Select League* baseball, Matt chose camp. When it came down to choosing high school football or the Attic Band at church, Matt hung up his cleats and took up his guitar. When his school friends were, shall we say, doing a little partying, Matt stayed home, telling us why only after we asked him why he wasn't hanging out with his "buds."

So, Why Matt?

Given the pool of candidates, why wouldn't God take one of the many whose life was pointing to certain destruction anyway? Why take a stellar young man who saw surrender to God as a high calling, not a sign of weakness?

Whyville is an ugly place. By that I mean that it can bring ugly ideas out of us. I eventually realized that those "other types" of young people had loved ones, too. It was incredibly unkind of me to harbor such selfish thoughts.

Yep— *Whyville* is a very ugly place.

Juneau, the capital of Alaska, is a small, but stunningly beautiful city situated between the Gulf of Alaska and some of the most forbidding terrain imaginable. Huge mountains form its eastern border and deny nearly all access to the state's interior.

The city is laid out in a grid pattern, and all the streets begin and end at either mountains or water. No streets lead out of town. Everything needed for daily living is brought in by boat or plane, including the cars that travel up and down the city streets. You could drive all day long in Juneau, but never leave town—like being trapped in an old episode of *The Twilight Zone*.

Whyville is exactly like that.

There is no way out by rationalizing or any other effort. The "town" contains a series of twists, turns, and dead ends. And, despite your best efforts, you will never see the city limit signs in your *rearview* mirror.

Life is filled with a seemingly endless litany of questions. Many can be answered. Others are dismissed. Yet others are rationalized away. And some just sit and glare at us, defying any clear answer. They are stubborn and unyielding.

I was again reminded of that holy moment in the surgery waiting room on Christmas Eve. And I realized again that, though *Whyville* is indeed a place of relentless questioning, there is only one question that really matters. Strip away the hurt and the tears and you will find that only this query remains:

Do I trust God, or not?

Not, "Do I understand?" Not, "Do I agree?" Not, "Can I take this anymore?" And certainly not, "Why Matt?" Just, "Do I really trust God, or not?"

Once again, it seemed as if time had stopped with me. I was back in that Ozark cornfield, with its trodden path through the middle. I remembered that I had made it through before—and I could make it again.

I already knew God was faithful. I knew He loved me. I knew He would never leave me. Nothing is outside His knowledge, will, or control.

And He can be trusted.

Somewhere around this time, I realized that it was a good idea to keep that small brown bottle, the one for my tears, close to me at all times. There were a few more tears to catch. I could almost hear God continue whispering to me:

"I'm big enough for all of your questions."

CHAPTER 11

The Definition of Despair

THE APARTMENT

My best guess is that Shaunda and I were together for only about three months in all of 2008. She spent most of her time at either the hospital hotel or the apartment. I was there on days off, vacation days, or any other time I could work things out to be with her.

During the periods of remission between treatments, we were at home in Greenville. During the periods of relapse, she was always at Matt's side. She is a strong believer in

Christ, an unbelievable wife, and a wonderful mother. Like any good mother would do, she rarely left Matt's side during the entire journey. When she did, it was usually against her will and involved the occasional kicking and screaming. On the few weekends I actually managed to get her home, she would sleep for a while and then get up, feeling guilt for not being by Matt's side.

Matt knew this, of course. We talked about it. Occasionally, he even got a little weary of her being so close at hand. Yet, he never asked her to leave. He seemed to understand that she needed to be there—perhaps more than he needed her there. Shaunda is the personification of selflessness.

With Matt's cancer now back with a vengeance, additional chemotherapy was administered. It was painfully obvious that the cycle was repeating itself. The rickety rollercoaster was climbing another steep hill. These secondary hills, like those on a rollercoaster, were not as steep, but we were coming to them faster.

Matt's first stem cell transplant had actually been fairly routine. A second would be experimental. So, we had to have an uncomfortable conversation with the transplant doctor. We faced the possibility that insurance might not cover a second transplant for Matt. It would be an experimental procedure, and expenses were already approaching the policy's million-dollar cap.

Cancer is not only a fearful thing—it is also very expensive.

One again, I was gripped by fear. We discussed funding options with the doctor and his nurse, in the event the insurance did indeed deny coverage. They were very sympathetic and informative. They told me that I would need to deposit $50,000 in cash for them to begin the process.

Now, I am not a wealthy man, but after crunching the numbers the shock eased a bit. "Let's see," I calculated, "the value of my house, less what I owe, minus the real estate commission, and plus the small amount of cash on hand—yes, I could pull this off."

That thought process helped to beat back the looming despair, at least for a moment. Then I noticed that the nurse's lips were still moving. I have no idea what I missed, but I well remember what I heard her say next.

"And then", she continued, "we'll have to figure out how you will pay the remainder of the nearly *two hundred thousand dollars...*" Her lips continued to move after that as well, but I heard no more words.

"Two hundred thousand dollars? Really?" Darkness was closing in all around me and it forced me into an abyss deeper than I had ever known. At that moment, I learned the true definition of despair—and I was in its suffocating grip.

I was not Matt's biological father, but he was fully my son, and I would gladly have sold my house and given everything I had to give him a shot at life. I would do anything I could, but that kind of money was far beyond my reach. I was being asked to do what I knew I could not do.

In that moment of genuine despair, I once again asked and answered the crucial question, "Would I trust God or not?" I chose at that moment to trust Him, yet again— this time with the *impossible*. But the worst case scenario never came. The insurance carrier ultimately agreed to pay for the second—experimental—transplant.

The lesson? ***Despair is the polar opposite of faith. I must never allow it to rule my life.***

I was on yet another trip on that awful rollercoaster. But I could no longer feel the wind blowing through my hair. It was no longer a sunny warm day. In fact, the gray Autumnal skies seemed to portend much darker things to come.

I was beginning to hate rollercoasters.

CHAPTER 12

But Who Will Hold My Arms Up?

I assure you that I am not, nor will I ever be an expert on the subject of grief. I am merely a sojourner on the path of suffering. However, I have learned a few things along the way. Although I cannot fully explain it, I know that, at least in general terms, women and men grieve differently.

Shaunda and I did.

From the time we assume our roles as husbands and fathers, we are "fixers." It's who we are and what we do.

When the chain falls off the bicycle sprocket, the parts roll our way. We pull out the tools and fix it.

And along the way, we tend to become quite self-reliant. *"Don't bother me with the map, or the GPS, or that crazy app on your phone. I already know how to get there. I need no assistance. Navigation is in my DNA."*

Then reality shows up.

It is quite difficult for some of us men to admit that there are things we can't fix. *"There must be something wrong with the replacement part. Call a repairman? No way. Are you kidding? Directions? Nope. To do that I must first admit I am lost. Sorry honey, no can do.*

It's not that I want to be dishonest. It's not that I think I can pull one over on you. I know I just don't have the skills in my wheelhouse to fix everything. And I know when I am hopelessly lost, and that we *will* likely run out of gas on a deserted highway.

Just don't expect me to admit it—*ever.*

I may be oversimplifying things, but it does beg the question: Why would a man go to such lengths to *not* say something? Here's why. I'm afraid of being too honest and transparent. I'm fearful you will discover that I have genuine weaknesses and that once you discover them, you will not respect me. And if you don't respect me, I fear you will not *love* me. Yet, all the while I know you see right through me.

And I dare complain that *you* are hard to understand?

Now you know why our major male communication techniques consist of fist bumps, high fives, and nicknames like "Bubba." We can't say "I really need to pour out my heart to you or I'm going to lose my mind." Nope. We say, "Hey Bubba, let's grab a burger and let off some steam." And without saying a word, a buddy will know that these two statements mean *exactly* the same thing.

While going through tragedy, we are sometimes afraid to face the reality that there are things we cannot fix. I must admit that I am clueless about where this journey will end. And I fear that I will run out of gas and lead my family to a horrible dead-end on some deserted highway.

And what's more, I can't tell you these things. I must remain faithful to God and continue to trust Him. I must tell any contrary thoughts and feelings to go back to hell where they belong.

If I find it hard to tell my wife these things because I fear I am inadequate as a communicator, I must find someone who understands this sense of inadequacy. This doesn't mean I don't love her, and if I'm smart, I'll figure out the right way to say these things to *her*. The last thing I need to do is to go dark with my wife.

Get ready for the high fives and fist bumps. *"Hey Bubba, I mean sweetheart, let's grab a burger."*

ENTER THE THREE MUSKETEERS (OR THREE AMIGOS, OR EVEN THE THREE STOOGES)

There is a great story in the Book of Exodus chapter 17. Moses told Joshua to fight the Amalekites, a group of people who had just attacked the Israelites. Joshua obeyed immediately. Moses stood atop a nearby hill, watching and commanding, while Joshua battled in the valley. As long as Moses held his staff in the air, the Israelites had the advantage. Whenever Moses dropped his hands, and therefore the staff, the Amalekites gained the advantage. And when they did, Moses witnessed his people being slaughtered.

I am not suggesting that as long as I held my hands up, Matt would win his battle—or if I dropped my hands he would lose it. But, I was in my *own* battle, as was every member of my family.

And just like Moses, I was getting weary. Let's see what happened to Moses:

Moses' arms soon became so tired he could no longer hold them up. So Aaron and Hur found a stone for him to sit on. Then they stood on each side of Moses, holding up his hands. So his hands held steady until sunset. As a result, Joshua overwhelmed the army of Amalek in battle. Exodus 17:12, 13 NLT

When Moses was just too tired to carry the load by himself, God sent two other men to help him. All three shared in the victory. You see it was not Moses's arms in the air that brought the advantage—it was what was in his hands at the end of his arms.

It was the staff of God.

As long as Moses's arms (and thus the staff) were raised, the battle turned toward Israel. When his arms dropped, the battle turned against them. It was the same for me. As long as I focused on God and the big picture, I was winning. But when I allowed despair to reign, I would begin to lose the battle. It's just that I'm not Moses. Two men would never be enough.

It would take three.

Three men were sent by God to help me in my battle. They listened without judgment, gave without any expectation of return, and loved without restraint. And they did so month after month.

Sometimes it was a simple text message. Other times a phone call. And occasionally it was a "whisk away" lunch that brought a few minutes of sanity. And often it was literally hours spent by my side in waiting rooms. They missed work, left their jobs on many occasions, and even used their vacation days to drive to Dallas just to sit and talk.

They would be part of this journey with me from inception to conclusion. Each one functioned independently and unknown to the others, yet each one had been there that *first* Christmas Eve. They would do anything I asked of them, including some pretty difficult things.

They were listening ears and shoulders on which to cry. They found things to make me laugh and never looked down on me when I cried. The three of them were from completely different spheres of my life. With the exception of one cold sunny March morning in 2009, I don't think I ever saw all three of them together other than on that first Christmas Eve.

MY FAMILY

I have been in the ministry for more than thirty years. I'll be honest, I have served in some churches where I felt that some of those in attendance each week really wished I would just move on down the road. I've also had the privilege to minister in churches where I honestly felt I was serving among friends. The latter has certainly been the case for me in Greenville.

I will mention very few names because I am certain I would leave someone out. I truly have no idea how much money was placed in my hand or slipped into my pocket. I never talked about financial needs—privately or publicly. I didn't think it was right or fair to do. I have witnessed many people who were in genuine need through the years. I have also seen many others who were, what we might call, "professionally needy," working the system for financial gain. I didn't wish to be in need at all. After all, I was called to serve these people, not to be served *by* them. Left unspoken was the fact that for more than a year I funded the equivalent of two households—our primary family home and the apartment. Of course, the apartment was much cheaper, a mere $600 per month plus a few bills. But things were tight. Yet through the entire journey I never once got behind in any of my financial obligations.

The co-pay on just one of Matt's many prescriptions was $400. But I never shared that fact with anyone. I only share it now, years later, so I may also share the testimony about the enormity of what God did.

Recently, I met a gentleman between our two Sunday morning services. He was coming down the stairs from the balcony, and I was entering the side sanctuary door. He held out his hand. As we exchanged pleasantries, I was immediately transported back to a time more than three years earlier—to another Sunday morning when that same man had shaken my hand. That morning, his handshake contained six crisp one hundred dollar bills. I will not mention his name, but here's something he doesn't know. The very next week, I stood at the window of the pharmacy at the hospital in Dallas. I smiled when the pharmacist apologetically asked for one more of those $400 co-pays. "It's no problem," I replied as I reached into my pocket and pulled out four of those crisp bills.

I had to keep my job. I had recurring bills to meet. I also felt I needed to be with Shaunda as much as possible. Truth be told, it was probably more important for me to be with her than with Matt. Software for web-based worship made it possible to do much of my work *remotely*. It was a Godsend.

This could easily become the longest portion of this book. Add to these, all the folks who washed our clothes, mowed our lawn, took care of our house, and a hundred other things. So much was done for us and given to us by our church family—staff and congregants—that I could spend the rest of my career in Greenville, and never be able to say "thank you" enough.

MY FAMILY

That's not a typo. I realize this section is titled just like the last, but this time it is about Shaunda's family. My parents passed away many years ago. I have a few family members that I still keep in touch with, but they are scattered around several states.

Shaunda's family, on the other hand, is large and awesome—doing the laundry, helping clean the house, showing up at all hours whenever there was need. One of Shaunda's cousins will always be known by us as the *Jason's Deli* angel. She showed up with great food so many times—including that first Christmas Eve morning.

With all of that being said, I'm going to run the risk of offending someone, yet this person's sacrifice for Matt begs to be told.

For me, life had turned into an uneasy routine. Work at the church Mondays and Tuesdays. Go home, sleep for an hour, take a shower, put on my uniform and work the street in warrant service those same nights. Work at the church Wednesday till noon, work warrants in the office all Wednesday afternoon, take a shower, change clothes and go back to the church for rehearsal Wednesday night. Work Thursday at the church and leave right after work for the hospital. Work warrants and church work all weekend via a laptop and cell phone, often from Matt's bedside. Stay with Matt at night when needed so Shaunda could get some sleep. Get up early Sunday morning and drive to church for early rehearsal. Leave right after the worship services and drive back to Dallas. Spend that night at the apartment, then get up early Monday morning to drive to the church for work.

Then repeat.

After several months of this schedule, to say the least, I was physically, spiritually, and mentally exhausted. I did, however, derive a temporary benefit.

I was too busy to *think*.

Into this equation for inevitable disaster enters Uncle Steve, once more. Steve is a staff pastor at our church and is married to Shaunda's sister. As such, he and I both had Fridays off. Somewhere in the flow of this crazy year, Steve announced that he was giving his day off to Matt. Every Thursday evening Steve walked away from his other responsibilities. He stayed with Matt every Thursday night and all day Friday. Sometimes into Saturday too—for months.

Steve could talk to Matt about anything. For that matter, Steve can talk to *anyone* about anything. The guy has the gift of gab. Matt told me often how he looked forward to Steve's visits and how they would talk for hours, sometimes all night. Steve has an infectious way about him. He can fill a room with laughter. He would usually just say "Hi Uncle Joe" and then walk right past me already discussing some nonsensical Dallas Cowboys play with Matt, or something from a Rangers or Maverick's game. Matt would smile and sit up a little straighter in the bed. They spoke of football and basketball, nonsense and relationships, and living and dying. I would just quietly slip out of the room.

Thank you Uncle Steve for going places few would dare to tread. In addition to being a vital support to your nephew, your visits gave me two incredible gifts.

First—a real day off. My routine was now broken by the ability to take my wife out of the environment that held her captive, if only for a while. We went to breakfast, we went to the mall, we went for coffee, and to the grocery store. We spent every Friday night at the apartment *together*. I have tried so hard while completing this work not to speak for my children or for my wife. My Journey was not theirs. Theirs held its own unique pain and I dare not disrespect that with a flawed attempt at speaking in areas that I could never understand. I will risk it here though, and say that what Steve did for Shaunda will always be of unspeakable value to her as well.

Secondly, it gave me the time to think. Not that I wanted it, you understand, I enjoyed being busy. It was rather that I needed it. I had to face the harshness of the reality that surrounded me. Here's another valuable lesson I learned, this one the hard way. ***Filling your life with busyness does not make reality go away.***

Looking back, without these two gifts from my brother-in-law, I most certainly would have lost my mind, or at the very least I would have lost my way.

Throughout my ministry I have heard the question posed: "Who will be a pastor to the Pastor?" After all, the Pastor is supposed to be there for everyone during his or her time of need. And to be quite honest, I have really enjoyed that part of my job. I have been a Police Chaplain as well as a Pastor for a long time. My phone regularly rings at all hours of the night. I have often joked that when the phone rings at three in the morning at our house, no one flies into a panic. I just catch a sharp elbow to the ribs.

I must admit though, that on several occasions through the years I have pondered that same question. Who really does "pastor the Pastor?" I can tell you this; at least for this circumstance in this Church at this time in my life, the answer was simple.

Everyone.

How can I ever say thank you for that?

CHAPTER 13

The Third "R"

The year-long barrage of Holiday disasters was eclipsed only by our first Thanksgiving and our second Christmas. One thing is for certain, although it may seem odd, I was truly thankful on this first Thanksgiving. It was November 2008, and I was thankful that Matt was still with us. Whyville came around from time to time, but I had learned to send it screaming to its rightful place and instead I chose to appreciate every moment of every day.

With the second, experimental bone marrow transplant now a full six weeks behind us, Matt was once again obviously better. His color was good. He was acting like he felt better. Against all odds the powerful drug of hope was once again having its intoxicating effect on our family. Matt was back on the platform at church *again*. A quick review of past schedules shows that he was leading worship with tunes like "Mighty To Save," "Everlasting God," and "Blessed Be Your Name," as well as "You Never Let Go." We were preparing for another Holiday season, grateful for each day. The roller coaster was on the way down the hill one more time.

It shouldn't surprise you now when I say that Thanksgiving meant another trip to the doctor. After all, it *was* a Holiday. Shaunda and I were full of intoxicating hope on the way to Matt's checkup. It started with another round of testing. More of the "three letter thing," CAT and MRI and PET, and the ever-present round of blood work to see the magic numbers. There was really little doubt about the results of the blood work. You could see it in Matt's eyes. He was starting to feel good again.

With the morning's testing behind us, we waited to see Matt's transplant doctor. Finally whisked into the small room, Matt's infectious smile lit up the place. Blood test results in hand, his primary nurse almost bounced into the room that afternoon. "I can't give you the results Matt, the doctor has to do that, but I think you'll like them!"

Even if she hadn't said a word we would have known. Her smile mimicked Matt's.

Matt's doctor entered the room a great deal more joyfully than usual. The blood test results were back and they were off the chart. Matt's blood counts were higher than they had been any time in the past year. With less-than-guarded enthusiasm, the doctor announced that the experimental transplant, once a source of despair, had apparently worked beyond anyone's dreams. I fought back tears once again--for two reasons. First, I had been on this ride before, and second, "giddy" never looked really good on me. Besides, that small brown bottle must be getting close to full.

Matt and his doctor talked about going on the road with Matt as the object lesson and the doctor as the speaker. High fives all around. The Doctor and nurse left, closing the door behind them. Now all we had to do was wait on the three-letter test results, and then we could zip back to Greenville and get on with the business of planning the Thanksgiving celebration that was now certain to be the greatest ever.

This time the wait didn't seem all that long. We talked, we laughed, and we smiled. There was a lull in our conversation so it was quiet in the room when we heard a rather loud and uncharacteristic expletive that came from the hallway of the otherwise very professional office. Worse yet, we recognized the voice. It was Matt's doctor. I feel quite certain that we all felt the same dark dagger of fear that pierced my chest.

The door opened again, this time much more slowly. Doctor and nurse re-entered, reluctantly. I don't think I'll finish this story; It still hurts me too badly to recount it and I think you get the idea anyway. I did realize that day that Matt's doctor and nurse had made a critical mistake on their end of the Practitioner/Patient relationship. I knew that at some point in the journey they had begun to genuinely care about Matt. For this gift, that I realize cost them dearly, I will also be forever grateful.

As you might have guessed, Thanksgiving Day was very quiet. You might say that we just "went through the motions" that day. I was, however, even more grateful to have that Thanksgiving with Matt than I had been the day before. Now I knew without any doubt that my initial impression, formed the preceding Christmas while looking at the first x-ray, was indeed correct. Matt would not be with us next Thanksgiving.

Hope is indeed a powerful drug and it is highly addictive. When one quits that "drug" cold turkey, it can cause excruciatingly painful withdrawal symptoms. The lesson? *Despair is a cruel master.* I can never make room for its icy clutches.

The third "R" now began to cut through my soul like a knife… reality.

CHAPTER 14

A Sad Story

Here's a sad story…

A lady was shopping on the day after Thanksgiving in 2008. After all, it was Black Friday. She saw a middle aged guy and his wife at a department store. The guy's wife found a jewelry chest that she just had to have, so they bought it. When the associate brought the boxed item to the sales floor, the man realized it wouldn't fit in their car. "He must not have given that much thought," the lady said to herself, "but it's the beginning of the Holiday season and I'm here in my husband's truck, so I'll help these poor ignorant folks!" She stepped forward with an offer, dropped the item off at their house and then drove away. She never saw the middle-aged couple again.

There it is, a sad story. Are you sad yet? I didn't think so. That's the story from the helpful lady's point of view. Here is the same story from another point of view.

Shaunda has drug me (that's a Texas term, used intentionally) shopping on the day after Thanksgiving every year we have been married. First it was to find bargains when money was very tight. Later it was more to watch the "shoppers" fight over $5 movies and $25 bicycles. On the day after this particular Thanksgiving, we went for neither of those reasons. We went because we had always gone, and we were trying desperately to hold our crumbling existence together. Matt was asymptomatic despite the recent bad news, so there was no reason not to "go through the motions" one more time, and that is what we did.

I remember that we walked aimlessly through a couple of our regular spots, purchasing nothing. I also remember that we spoke very little, each of us imprisoned by our own personal heartache.

It was still early, barely an hour had passed, so we headed west to the next town that held more shopping opportunities; as well as a different set of "shoppers." We walked through a couple more stores buying little, or perhaps nothing, and then decided to head back to

Greenville to go to breakfast at our favorite spot. We were both fighting despair... and the urge to just sit down in the middle of the store and cry.

Earlier that morning we discovered the "door-buster" deal of the day in one of the stores was a large, freestanding jewelry chest. I made an offhand comment wondering if it might double as a gun cabinet. A roll of the eyes from Shaunda, one that would make any young teenage girl proud, communicated clearly that continued silence was the best option. I did notice that it was the only time I had seen her show interest in anything that morning, but I was in no mood.

As we turned to leave, we noticed that it had begun to rain–very hard. We dashed toward the car. Rain soaked and weary, and fighting despair with every step, I literally stopped dead in the middle of driving rain when I noticed the front tire was flat; cartoonishly flat.

We took shelter in the car and decided to wait out the rain, But as the icy fingers of despair took hold of my heart, I knew I could sit there no longer. In the driving rain, I exchanged the flat tire with the stowaway spare.

At some point during the 25-minute ride home, my hair dried enough to stop the water streaming into my eyes. Though drenched, I was still hungry. The fact that a national tire chain store shared a parking lot with our favorite restaurant was too convenient to pass up. I dropped the car off for a tire repair and we sloshed into the eatery.

With the exception of placing our orders, I'm not sure Shaunda or I spoke a word. I could not get the silly jewelry chest off my mind. I did however, dry out a bit, and it had quit raining. We picked up the car and, instead of turning right towards our house, I silently made a quick left towards our tiny mall. This dated shopping center held more empty spaces than stores, but it did have a much smaller version of the store that had the "doorbuster" deal on the jewelry chest. I was mustering as much Christmas spirit as I could.

This would have to be quick. Although Matt was not "sick" at this point, he would be waking up soon and we wanted to be there. We didn't want him to be alone–this was all we could really offer him.

I marched us both into the store over her protests, and, with much bravado, approached a sales associate, pointed at the floor model and announced, "I want one." Shaunda complained a bit, but not very much or very loudly.

For the first time that morning as I slapped down the plastic, I was feeling a bit of life course through my veins. Just a little mind you, and it went flying out the double glass doors of the store when an associate appeared with a large boxed item, way too large to ever fit in a car. Now I just felt foolish. How could I be so naïve? Why was I so rash? Who did we know that was in town and had a pickup?

The sales associate walked away leaving us alone in the aisle. We spoke quietly together. The enormity of the day, the rain, the flat tire, the stupidity, and the cancer pushed me once again to the absolute edge of despair.

At that moment a lady we did not know walked up. "You can't get that in your car, can you?"

A quick search for a clever response yielded only a sheepish smile and a "No, actually, I can't."

She went on to tell us that she'd had to take her husband's truck that morning. It had been parked behind her car and she dared not wake him at that early hour. She would be happy to carry our purchase to our home for us.

With the difficulty now resolved, the sales associate reappeared. He offered the use of a hand truck and we placed the item in the bed of our newfound friend's truck. The short trip to the house was over in a moment and the bulky gift was unloaded, and our new friend was gone.

When I said "thank you" yet again, she told me it was not a big deal and I assured her that she had no idea how big a deal it was. To her, it was a small act of kindness. To me, it was an act of God. To me it was a reminder that God was taking care of me, even in the very smallest of things.

For the first time that day I cried. For the first time that day I smiled.

Sad story? Not for me. It is rather a story of love, hope, and faithfulness. "So what's so sad about it?" you ask.

The sad story is found in how many times we find ourselves so self-absorbed that we walk right by those who are in need, never having seen them.

Was it "no big deal," as the lady said? Truth is, we have no idea what another human being is going through. Perhaps they find themselves, by virtue of their journey, balancing perilously on the edge of despair, or even sanity. Their life might be forever changed by a kind word or a simple deed.

Instead we shrug, walk away and do nothing. Now *that* is a sad story.

CHAPTER 15

To Don'ts

I can tell you for certain that I do not know, nor do I believe I will ever feel, that I am qualified to write a "to do" book on grief or loss. It's not that I haven't discovered some things that worked, for me at least, because I did. I also tried a lot of things that didn't work. My precious wife was very forgiving then; she just seemed grateful that I was trying. Other folks might not be so forgiving.

Unfortunately however, I have experienced some real "to don'ts." and I don't mind sharing those at all. Here are four things we experienced that really didn't work.

Maybe I can spare another family some pain, or at least get an "amen" from a reader.

HOW ABOUT A NIGHT OUT?

Guess I'll start with me. This one was my very own "to don't." I didn't need any help with this one. I managed to mess it up all by myself. When that first Valentine's Day rolled around, we were, as you might already have guessed, at the hospital while Matt was undergoing a round of chemo.

We were early in the journey and Shaunda needed a night out, or at least so I surmised. I would make it a good one, something memorable. She seemed pretty discouraged at the time, so it did not surprise me when she balked a bit when, without warning, I drove her to the nearest mall to buy a dress.

I picked out a beautiful formal red dress. She didn't have anything remotely like it, so I thought it was perfect. OK, so sometimes guys think a bit backwards. Hmmm, now that I think about it, maybe there was a reason she didn't have anything remotely like it. I asked Shaunda's mother to come and stay with Matt so I could "whisk Shaunda away." Dressed in my best suit, with Dallas Symphony tickets in hand we paraded out the front doors of the hospital into the waiting car.

After a fine dinner, most of which I recall that Shaunda didn't eat, we were off to the Meyerson, our local venue for the Dallas Symphony Orchestra. The music was outstanding. The auditorium was elegant. My beautiful "date" in the red dress was breathtaking, at least by all outward appearances. On the inside though, she was miserable.

We returned to the hospital having spoken few words. Shaunda was very gracious and appreciative; it's just that I had apparently taken her to the last place in the world she wanted to go and at the worst possible moment. As a matter of fact, anywhere *except* the hospital was the last place she wanted to go. Later on, she would enjoy a few minutes away. At that moment however, I was merely keeping her from doing what she really needed, and desperately wanted, to do.

To be quite honest, at the time I honestly didn't get it. What had I done wrong? I choose not to make myself look any more foolish at this point by providing the answer to the question, which is already obvious to most everyone. I will instead share the lesson that I learned.

Be quiet and just listen. You are in territory that you do not understand. Needless to say, I did a lot of listening from that point on.

JUST A LITTLE MORE FAITH

None of us are really sure who he was. Throughout 2008, hundreds of people visited Matt, perhaps more than a thousand. This young visitor in particular was smartly dressed and overtly kind. His visit was concurrent with that of several of Matt's friends. Upon leaving, this visitor handed Matt what was obviously a Christian book and then said goodbye.

After he was gone, the conversation quickly turned to "Who was that guy anyway?" After a few minutes of discussion and more than a few chuckles, everyone agreed that no one knew him, not even Matt.

Later that evening, after all the visitors had left; Matt picked up the book the young man left and began to read. The book was written by a well-meaning Christian author. The premise of the book was disconcerting to all of us to say the least, and one with which I vehemently disagreed. The message of the book was simple. If you are sick, ask God to heal you. If God does not heal you, it is because you do not have enough faith.

I was raised in an entirely different type of Church than the one I now serve. As such, I am most likely a bit more tolerant of other Christian belief systems than the majority of my contemporaries. I was, however, not very tolerant of this one. As a matter of fact, I recall wishing that I had visited just a bit more with the young man who left Matt that book. I would have liked to thank him for his time and concern, and then taught him by example the definition of "righteous indignation."

Matt suffered physically. Matt had not been healed. Neither of these facts was the result of any "lack of faith" on Matt's part. Quite the contrary. Matt's dignity and respect for the will of God in his life, which, by the way, was expressing itself at a very great cost, was a sign of a depth of faith most will probably never know, likely including the smartly dressed young man.

IT'S OK IF I CRY

I have always been an emotional person. I have at times tried to hide it. I have at times tried to run from it. I was offered a third option from a good friend at one point during this journey.

I was bemoaning my tendency towards emotion to this friend in a very private conversation. I pointed out that it seemed really odd for me to be so easily moved, emotionally, and yet be a part of the law enforcement community. I was so different from most of the other officers.

"Different" he responded, "you bet you are." It seems that everyone I work with is pretty cold and calculated. "We don't need more people like them, there are plenty already. We need more like you. Don't run from how God made you, embrace it instead."

Embrace it? You've got to be kidding. Now "embrace it" does not mean, "Give in to its weaknesses," nor does it mean to use "this is just who I am" as an excuse. It means rather to accept yourself for how God made you, and embrace it as your baseline. Start from there and work to be the best Christian you can be instead of wasting your energy trying to pretend you are something you are not.

Throughout the journey there were those who had the ability to hit the issue of Matt's illness head on, and there were those who avoided it altogether. I learned through my years of serving as a Police Chaplain that the death of a family member doesn't mean you should act as though that person never existed at all. If a loved one was killed in a tragic car accident, you wouldn't run home and grab a pair of scissors and cut them out of every family picture you have. An unspeakable tragedy or untimely death does not mean that the person's life had no significance.

Don't be afraid of someone who is hurting. It's OK if they cry. The big "to don't" here: don't act like it never happened.

YOU SHOULD HAVE...

Everyone has an opinion. Throughout my ministerial career I have experienced hundreds of well-meaning opinions, and I'd like to think I've learned to do the most with them.

I have a secret. Well I *did* have a secret. After I tell you I guess it won't be a secret anymore. But for whatever reason, I have always struggled a bit with self-worth. That may be why I've never excelled at taking criticism. When I was first in the ministry, every negative opinion shared shook me to the core. I would typically respond in a fashion that would leave little doubt in anyone's mind that I was a pompous arrogant gasbag. But it was really only a smokescreen intended to hide the truth of my insecurity.

There is probably no more divisive segment in Church ministry that evokes more "opinions" than music. It seems that any given Sunday worship service is too loud, too slow, too contemporary, too quiet and too old fashioned, all at the same time. Music is perhaps the element most objected to in the Church, and often the most divisive. I have learned to take the useful information from the "opinions" of others, learn from them, then discard the rest. It is weakness to bend to every criticism, and arrogant to ignore them.

When it came to Matt's health care decisions, he was past the age of 18, so he got to make them all on his own. He took the advice of the doctors he trusted, but to the best of my knowledge, he never once asked my opinion concerning his Medical care. I don't think he ever asked anyone else's either. And to be quite frank, I was fine with that. I wouldn't have wanted the responsibility that accompanied those opinions.

We often laughed at ourselves when we asked a doctor a question and he merely smiled. "Can't answer that, sorry," or something similar was the inevitable response. "You're not the patient."

At this point in the journey, with reality now firmly in place, frustration was beginning to take its toll on all of us. Matt had acted on every medical opinion he received. He had endured two stem cell transplants and there was talk of a third. Everything was working and nothing was working. Every treatment beat back the cancer, but none could keep it from coming back. The cancer seemed to grow more aggressive with every passing day. It was also becoming painfully clear that it would not be satisfied until it stole my son's last breath. It was in the framework of this ever growing darkness that this final "to don't" appeared in the form of an unsolicited opinion.

You should have taken Matt to _ _ _ _ _. You can fill in the name of any cancer hospital or cancer treatment center you like, as long as it is not the one where you sought treatment.

I can't prove this, but I have come to believe that the following is true based on my years of experience with traumatic incidents. At some point in every such situation, nearly every person associated makes the incident somehow their own fault.

"If I hadn't gone to the store, he'd still be alive."

"If I had watched closer, she would have never taken her own life."

Some of these statements may have a shred of truth, but most do not. You would be surprised at the twisted logic

I have seen used to take responsibility for some event. It can deny all reason. I have come to believe that people do this to themselves as a sort of defense mechanism. If this thing that happened was my fault, it could have been stopped. it seems that guilt is a lesser burden to bear than powerlessness.

The "to don't" here is a little complex, but here it is. Don't assume responsibility or blame for things that you are powerless to control. And for sure don't transfer that blame to anyone else.

CHAPTER 16

A Lesson From The Darkness

I have told several people that there are parts of a journey like this that are so dark that they dare not ever be shared. This may be one of those stories. At any rate, it's close. It's just that the lesson learned here is too important *not* to share.

There are a lot of reasons people don't sleep, sometimes physical, sometimes emotional; sometimes even spiritual. Often it is simply because it is too noisy. When Matt was home during his illness, it was often noisy. He coughed a lot. A LOT. Not what is called a "productive" cough just a dry cough brought about by an unwelcome irritant in his chest. And Matt didn't cough every night, just most nights. He coughed when he was awake, and he coughed while he was asleep.

When he wasn't coughing, he was snoring. His snore was *loud*. House-shaking. Monumental.

Then, every once in a while and for no apparent reason, we would have a completely quiet night.

I was often unable to sleep when Matt snored and coughed. I usually left Shaunda in bed and wandered into the living room to watch a movie, play a video game or read a book. I tried to block out the seemingly constant noise from Matt's room, partly because it kept me awake, but mostly because it broke my heart to know he was suffering. The awareness that I would soon have to get up and go to work would eventually drive me back to bed and I would get a few hours of needed sleep.

During remission, Matt slept great. During relapse, it was more difficult. During the reality phase, it was terrifying.

On one particular occasion I woke up in the early hours of the morning. I lay very still, fighting to gain some sense, when I noticed two things. Shaunda was not in bed with me, and it was very quiet. I chose to take advantage of the quiet and rolled over to go back to sleep. Soon, though, my heart went out to Shaunda, so I rolled out of bed. I went to the living room where I assumed she was occupying my spot on the couch, but the couch was empty.

I walked into the kitchen to see if she was getting a glass of water, but she was not there either. I opened the door leading to the garage to see if her car was there, and it was. I was getting a bit concerned that maybe it was the rapture and I had missed it. (Told you I was groggy.)

I returned to the bedroom to retrieve my cell phone from its charging cradle. I used its faint light to search the rest of the house. That light afforded me a view of the hallway leading to Matt's room. It was there I found Shaunda. She was lying on the floor. No pillow, no covers, just lying on the floor, her head right next to Matt's bedroom door.

I walked quietly over to her, got down on my knees and leaned over, intending to whisper in her ear. I wanted to gently wake her up and see if I could encourage her to come back to bed. To my surprise, she was not asleep at all.

"What are you doing?" I asked in a hushed tone, most likely with less than the appropriate tenderness.

"Shhh," Shaunda replied. "It was too quiet. I just wanted to hear him breathe."

The noise kept me from sleeping. The silence kept Shaunda awake.

The lesson? This is one I would learn over and over during the remainder of the journey. The quietness and the darkness taught me that *there are things we can experience in this life that are far worse than death.*

CHAPTER 17

Oh, Yes, I Do

The countdown clock on the big screens clicked down to service start time. The band was to stage at two minutes to start time, the vocals at one minute. Matt filled both roles, and missed both deadlines. I left the platform and went to look for him. I was more than a bit concerned. It was one of the last Sundays he would be able to lead worship. Anyone who looked at him would assuredly have realized the same truth. I believe the worshippers that Sunday morning were quite aware that a life and death drama was playing out. They had watched Matt lead worship for weeks while his body dramatically changed in front of their eyes.

I found him in the hallway leading up to the platform area. I looked on the visage of a young man that somehow seemed to resemble my son less and less every week. His face and body had swollen from all of the steroids and taken on a ruddy complexion. His thick, dark hair was long gone. Legs wrapped around his acoustic guitar, his entire body rose and fell with every labored breath.

I still remember telling him that he "didn't have to go on" that day. And I still remember the four words he rather defiantly and slowly said back to me:

"OH, YES, I, DO."

And with that, Matt stood up and walked out on the platform and led the first song,

> *Blessed be your Name*
> *When the sun's shining down on me*
> *When the world's all that it should be*
> *Blessed be your Name.*
> *And then the second verse:*
> *Blessed be your name*
> *On the road marked with suffering*
> *When there's pain in the offering*
> *Blessed be your Name.*
> *The next song that day?*

No, no you never let go
Through the calm and through the storm
No, you never let go of me

The response to that worship sequence was a strange mix of tears, singing, applause, and shouting. It was heart rending. It was difficult. It was glorious. When the first set of songs was complete, I tell you the truth, I thought people were never going to quit applauding and shouting. I believe that they too understood the importance of what they had just witnessed. Matt just smiled. I just looked around to see if perhaps standing unnoticed in the crowd that day was Jesus himself.

When the applause finally died down, the drummer gave four clicks and Matt began a familiar rhythm. I have no idea where the other worshippers were in their hearts and minds that day. I do however, remember where I was. I was standing in front of Matt's bedroom door during that made-for-TV movie. I was listening. Listening to the first time I heard him sing those words. I was just then realizing that somehow through the lyric of this song his young life was coming full circle.

I reached for that small bottle to find if there was room for any more tears as Matt once again sang the first line:

The splendor of a King
Clothed in majesty
Let all the world Rejoice...
How great is our God.

Matt had come to understand even at his young age that *the ability to weather life's storms and the choice to worship in spite of them were inexorably linked.* Dealing with the difficulties of our journey is made immeasurably easier by a total refusal to hate God, replaced instead with a dogged determination to proclaim as Job did..."Though He slay me, I will trust in Him."

In our journey, there was no one to blame but God. Matt didn't die because another person chose to drink and drive. We didn't lose him because of an addiction, a life choice, or because he became disillusioned with life. Bottom line, Matt died because God chose to let it happen. At any time He could have said "enough" and made our nightmare disappear.

But He didn't.

He instead chose to allow the worst to happen.

In your loss, you may be able to blame alcohol, drugs, smoking, friends, war, violence or any of a thousand other things. But if you look deeper, past the surface reasons, you'll find that God is a part of your picture as well. Was your child killed by a drunk driver? Certainly alcohol can be a factor, but why did God allow your child to be the one that was on that particular stretch of highway at that time? It's God's fault.

Perhaps your lifelong partner died of lung cancer. It was those cigarettes that did it. Those "cancer sticks." That filthy habit. The big tobacco companies who make certain that a highly addictive drug is included in every puff. And there is some truth in all of these statements. Yet millions of people have smoked and then died in their eighties or nineties. Why did God permit your loved one to become a statistic?

Many others languish for years in what is, perhaps, the most destructive of all thought processes: It was *my* fault. If only I had been a better mom, my child would not have taken his own life. Had I been a better dad, perhaps my son would have never felt the need to use drugs. Ultimately, if you follow this debilitating spiral to it's inevitable conclusion, it will eventually end with God. If I had been a better person, God would not have punished me with the loss of my child.

All of these attempts to navigate the cornfield end with one of two conclusions: God is a vengeful, cruel being at worst, or entirely aloof and unconcerned at best. May I submit that there is a third, Biblical conclusion that we can reach? A conclusion that drives us to our knees in front of a loving, holy God?

Here it is. God is God and I am not. His ways are not my ways, they are higher than mine. His thoughts are not my thoughts, they are higher than mine. God has a purpose for everything, although I may never grasp it while I breathe the good air of this earth. There is no such thing as random chance in spite of how circumstances may appear. After you realize and accept that all of this thing we call "life" is really all about God, you will be faced with an awesome, life-changing choice. Will you let God off the hook, or hold him responsible until your last bitter breath? When God takes the best, will you give Him glory?

Don't worry. He's not God because you voted Him in, so you can't vote Him out. You didn't make Him God; no-one did, He was God already and He was God all by Himself. You can surely break His heart, but you can't make Him stop being God. He doesn't serve at our pleasure; we are to serve at His. When you reach the end of your bitterness, you will discover that He is still God, and that He stands there with open arms to receive you back to Himself. Then, wrapped in the arms of forgiving grace, you will discover that He is a great big God; big enough for your questions too.

It was at this very critical point of the journey that Matt found himself on that Sunday morning so near the end. As the countdown clock ticked away the seconds that marked the beginning of the service, it was just as surely counting down the last days of Matt's life. When faced with this horrible truth, with enormous effort Matt stood to his feet, strapped on his guitar, and made it onto the stage. He had made his choice with those four resounding words: "Oh, yes, I do."

Keep in mind we don't worship God because He is good to us. Plainly said, I don't really like everything that God does, but, again, that is not because I think He's mean, but rather because I don't understand. You see, I am not God. He is higher; much higher. Don't misunderstand, gratitude is a commendable and, frankly, the expected response to our God, but not the *reason* we worship. Here's a powerful lesson: ***We don't worship God because He is good, we worship God because He is God***, all by Himself without anybody's help or proclamation. The crucial question here is not "Do you approve of Him," but rather "Do you trust Him."

CHAPTER 18

Merry Christmas Again

(And I've got the picture to prove it!)

As 2008 rolled on, Matt continued with his Chemo treatments only they were now supplemented with radiation therapy. The addition of radiation brought with it a brand new symptom for Matt, he was now getting progressively sicker. Yep, *that* kind of sick. Please let me remind you that Matt's cancer was so different, so aggressive. It came on and took him down so fast that it was unlike anything I had ever seen. Matt was never emaciated in the way we think of a cancer patient being emaciated. That is partly why the roller coaster ride was so intense. And for the record, I chronicled only a few of those roller coaster experiences in this work. Truth be told, there were many more.

Matt and I had laughed several times over the preceding months about how he had done what I could not do that first Christmas, getting all the family together at one time for Christmas. The kids were grown and spread out from Texas to Chicago to West Virginia. Getting together was not an easy thing, yet Matt had pulled it off. It seemed as if he was intent on doing it again this year as well. Christmas 2008 was now just around the corner.

I have learned a great lesson about Holidays in the past few years. This lesson came from a combination of raising a blended family and having your children grow up and begin their own lives. Successful Holidays are not truly date specific; they are more about when you can all get together. Foolish is the person who pressures his loved ones to gather on a specific day. With a little planning, a great Holiday experience can bounce around the calendar a bit. Like celebrating the fourth of July on the third, or having Thanksgiving dinner on the Sunday before Thanksgiving. Such would be the case on our second Christmas of the journey. The myriad of schedules would not permit gathering on Christmas Eve or Christmas Day, but they would permit an "all together" Christmas celebration a week earlier.

And so it was planned. Everyone seemed to happily cooperate, even Matt—though he was getting sicker by the day. We offered to take him back to the hospital multiple times, but he refused. I'm not certain if he desperately wanted to have a family Christmas, or if he just wanted *me* to have a family Christmas. Truthfully, it was probably both. So once again we honored Matt's wishes.

It was hard to believe that it had been almost exactly one year earlier that we had completed that Christmas concert. Could it really have been just one year? Nothing we knew of was really "wrong" then. It was almost like a different lifetime, sometimes even like someone else's lifetime.

The day finally came and all of the family gathered. Jodi, Ben and Makenna (the most precious granddaughter in the world), Lynn, Joey, Matt, Lauren, Shaunda, and me. Shaunda has long been an expert in cooking for the kids. Her philosophy? Find every possible form of junk food and make it available along with a healthy assortment of hummus, fruit, and vegetables.

After dinner we talked, shared memories, and laughed, literally for hours. We passed around old pictures and each shared stories of their latest adventures. Even a casual glance into Matt's eyes revealed an unexpressed agony just under the surface, yet all night his face radiated with that same infectious smile we had come to love through the years.

Other family members stopped by, sharing our moment together, and lingered. It seemed as if no one really wanted to leave. I guess we really didn't.

When it became obvious that the evening was drawing to a close, someone shouted above the crowd, "Get the camera!" Amid loudly expressed objections, all the kids gathered in front of the fireplace for the obligatory family picture.

As the kids smiled and said "cheese" (corny, I know), the room grew strangely quiet. It was as if everyone realized at the same moment the significance of what had just happened. We all knew what that picture meant, including Matt. And we all acknowledged at that moment that it could never happen again.

The laughter quickly faded away and turned into tears. Everyone shared hugs and expressed genuine I love yous. One by one they all said goodbye, and it was finally just Shaunda, Matt, and me left at the house. One final time we asked Matt if he wanted us to take him to the hospital. "Not yet," he replied, and he quietly slipped off down the hall to his room.

Neither Shaunda nor I slept at all that night. Mostly I remember holding each other very tightly in the darkness. Before the sun rose, Matt walked into our room and simply said, "It's time."

We all knew what that meant. Without saying more than the essential words we both got dressed. Shaunda grabbed the small overnight bag that she always kept packed and ready by the bed.

With moonlight glistening off the hood of the car, and the stillness of that cold winter night enveloping all of us down to our souls, we quietly got into the car for that 49 mile trip one more time.

Only two of us would return. Looking back, I think we all knew that as well.

PART 3
Tears in A Bottle

CHAPTER 19

A Million Reasons

It's another one of those times that "they say"... hmmm, seems like a lot of life is figuring out what "they" say and who "they" really are. Nevertheless, it is said that recovery begins only when you accept the truth. Unlike the others in this story, I accepted the truth on the very first day. I saw the x-ray. I knew that unless God performed a "red sea" caliber miracle, that Matt's illness was not survivable. For everyone else, the acceptance came more slowly, for some not until the last few weeks or even days. Then it rushed in like the storm surge leading an impending hurricane.

It was during this time that we were the most vulnerable.

We had long fought the journey to ICU. When you spend the better part of fourteen months in and around a hospital, you tend to learn the ins and outs of the daily routine. You also get a front row seat to the downward health spiral that often accompanies cancer. It is there that you learn how few really recover. You also learn that the journey to ICU can be a journey of no return.

Watching "cancer commercials" on television still makes me angry. They portray images of people that are winning the battle. Now I understand what they are doing; I probably understand it too well. They are in the business of selling the hope drug. People who are facing the imminent loss of a loved one are in the market for hope. People who have lost those family members often prefer a more honest approach. I know we do, and we did then, as well. Although there was plenty of "hope" marketed to us, our relationship with Matt's medical team was also full of reality. For this I now find myself somehow strangely and unexpectedly grateful.

I have never been a wealthy man. I can play the piano a bit and make a little music, but I also chose the Ministry path. That seemed to assure that I would stay away from substantial income. As such, I cannot even fathom what a million dollars would look like, or a million "anythings" for that matter. One of our Deputies seized just over $550,000.00 of drug money from a vehicle stop one night. That was an impressive sight to be sure; all that cash laid out on a folding table, but it was still well short of a million.

You might only imagine how it feels to get a letter from the business office of your son's medical team stating that his insurance cap had now been met; a million dollars. This was barely one month before Matt's eternal graduation day.

I will not go into the details of this side trip because it would be misunderstood by nearly everyone. I believe it is enough to say that *everyone* involved eventually did the right thing by Matt. I am grateful for this as well. Everyone that is, except for one doctor. This was only a few days before Matt died. He would soon be in ICU.

That third "R," Reality, was the key word that best describes these final bleak days. It was as if someone had turned off all the music and laughter in the world, and there remained only a painful, ever encroaching silence. It was no longer the realization that this required a miracle. It was the realization that it required a miracle right now. It was only then that we met the doctor who was the head of the stem cell program. We had seen him pass by many times, but we had never met him face to face. He was not a part of Matt's direct treatment team, at least to our knowledge. But now in the small ICU waiting room, he requested to meet with Matt's mom. Thank God, I was there too.

I knew this would be neither pleasant nor easy; but I believed I knew what was coming. Unfortunately I was correct. Yet the approach this man used shocked even me. For the sake of my family, and my own memories, I will not describe Matt's physical condition in detail at all. It is enough to say that he was in very bad shape. Funny, but this meeting seemed to correspond with the million-dollar notice from the insurance company. It was around these circumstances that this doctor suggested we stop treating Matt altogether and spend our money instead on a vacation with him.

I hope that statement shocked you like it shocked me that afternoon. Now don't misunderstand, there are times when I believe that advice is absolutely correct. As a matter of fact, during my 30 years in the ministry I've shared similar advice. It was not wrong advice, just the wrong time. As a parent, I could not (and still cannot) separate this conversation from the fact that the insurance well had just dried up. I never raised my voice; I never said a curse word. Instead I tried to respond with the same grace I had seen in Matt for the preceding fourteen months. I assure you though; I expressed *my* opinion about *his* opinion.

To this day I wonder if he had ever really met my son. I wonder if he ever looked into his eyes, or rather just looked at a written report, chart or lab test result. I wonder if there were inter-office politics at play, or if he were pressured from some financial decision makers above him. I will never know.

I did learn however, that *sometimes there can be a million reasons to make a right decision, but it has nothing to do with a dollar.* Besides, even an ignorant preacher with no medical training at all could tell that there was no real treatment going on, and most likely none that would ever take place. It was only the medical community offering what they could to show mercy in the onslaught of a faceless tyrant bent on taking Matt's last breath. Matt was in no condition to even consider a family vacation. He would have never survived the trip to the car.

Regardless, this fifteen-minute meeting caused me great distress. There was still talk of a third transplant and aggressive chemotherapy. And who could really say. As fast as the cancer came on, and then abated, we didn't know what to think. Keep in mind, the medical decisions concerning Matt's care were not mine, they were his. Matt still had some fight in him. In between greatly labored breaths Matt assured us he did not want to give up. In response to Matt's desire to fight, his primary transplant doctor chose to fight as well. How could I do any less? Yet someone whose name I didn't know and face I didn't recognize was trying to take the fight away.

I know another gentleman who by the very nature of his profession and life is a man of considerable influence. He is a physician and from all outward appearance, he is a moral man, and a Godly man. He served as an elected state official and He also has proved to be my friend.

On at least two occasions I received strange phone calls from him. He regularly called and checked on Matt, although Matt was not really his patient at this time. On both of these strange occasions however, spread out over the year, he closed his calls with basically the same thought.

"Hey preacher," he said, "I know how you guys are. You need anything? I've got at least a little money. You need money Preacher? I'll help you, you know. No one will ever have to know."

Now I've had all different kinds of doctors ask *me* for money, but I'd never had any *offer* me money before. I was dumfounded to say the least. I was being taken care of by our "families," so I graciously declined his offer.

"Anything you need Preacher, day or night. You've got my cell number. You call." And with that he would assure me of his prayers and say goodbye.

I was humbled to say the least, and I never took him up on his offer for help… until that moment. I was going to fight alongside Matt as long as he wanted to continue the fight, regardless of whether it made sense or not. I owed him that.

I reached for my cell phone and called my doctor friend. I'm not certain what I sounded like as I tried to explain. I told him that I knew the insurance money was gone. The third "R," reality, was now firmly in place. I knew, short of a direct intervention of Almighty God, that this journey would be over quite soon. Yet, I was going to honor Matt's wishes and we would continue the fight. Yet there seemed to be an internal conflict amongst the doctors on whether to continue or not.

I hung up the phone and went back to the hospital room where Matt lay struggling to breathe. I closed the door. I'll always remember his smile when I entered the room. We sat quietly for a few minutes.

Now I do not know exactly what my friend did, whom he called, or if he did anything at all. I only know that in less than thirty minutes there was a knock on Matt's door. A smartly dressed gentleman about my age entered the room. I do not remember his name, but I do remember that he introduced himself as a member of the board of directors of the hospital. His manner was confident. He was incredibly gracious, overtly compassionate, and very well spoken.

After introducing himself to Matt and me, he started his visit with "Young man, I understand you are quite a fighter." The next few moments were some of the most encouraging and at the same time the most direct we had experienced.

He spoke plainly about death, a conversation Matt and I had already had on several occasions.

He spoke plainly of finance, something I had shielded Matt from up to that point. He told Matt that his insurance had run out, but that there were "many ways to pay for things," and that Matt "need not worry."

He assured us that no matter the outcome, they would fight as long as Matt wanted to fight, regardless of the odds, *or* the dollars.

I really wanted to hug the man, not only for what he had just given Matt, but also for what he had just given our family, and it had nothing to do with money.

After a few minutes he shook Matt's hand. He motioned to me as he walked out the door. Outside of Matt's room, he shook my hand as well and assured me that he would do anything for us that he could, and he pledged the hospital's support as well. Choking back grateful tears I thanked him and he turned to walk away.

Only a few steps down the hallway, he turned back to me and smiled. "Mr. Knight," he said, "you certainly have some powerful friends." With that he smiled again and walked away.

Through my mind ran a cinema. Every person that had ever prayed for us was in the production as was every person who helped us financially. Our Church family and my "Three Musketeers." One by one our friends and family walked through my mind. They were followed by my doctor friend, and finishing the parade was Jesus Christ Himself.

"Powerful friends?" I thought almost aloud, "Sir, you have no idea." And with that I reentered Matt's room.

Matt was still smiling.

There would not be a third stem cell transplant.

There would not be a wedding.

As you have no doubt already guessed, the final outcome would soon be closest to scenario #2. It was the one I honestly expected all along, ever since that first day before Christmas when I saw the x-ray. It was what I had dreaded with all that was in me.

CHAPTER 20

I Will Never Forget

I will never forget the morning Matt died. It was still Saturday night when Shaunda and I went back to the tiny apartment next to the hospital. We thought we'd get a few hours of needed sleep. At this point Shaunda had been by Matt's bedside for days, and I had to catch a little sleep since the next day was Sunday. Shortly after midnight the phone rang. "Come back," Lauren said, "and hurry." I looked at my watch and I realized it was Sunday morning. Just as quickly, although I cannot explain it, I realized there was no need to hurry. How fitting. Sunday morning, and Matt was at home.

While our lives were blessed with many great doctors and nurses, there is one nurse that stands out above the rest; and I never knew her name. As a matter of fact, I don't think I ever saw her before, and certainly not since.

After Matt completed his journey home, there were some necessary, but uncomfortable duties that had to be completed to the flawed earthly house that had held him captive. There was some cleaning up, some removal of tubes and other tasks to be completed. God had one more angel to send our way. The kind, soft-spoken nurse we had never met before entered the ICU room to prepare Matt's body for its last journey.

After removing the medical implements and unhooking all the machines, she took a white washcloth and began tenderly washing Matt's face. What she did next though, is why I will always remember her.

The ICU for a cancer treatment center is a painfully quiet place. During the nights we had just spent, we heard very little noise with the exception of the various medical machines mindlessly going about their life prolonging duties. Talk was hushed, small talk was non-existent. The silence was eclipsed at unpredictable times by the soft cries and muffled sobs of others who were already at the place we did not want to go, but where we now were.

In my career I have worked with some great talent, but it was at that moment that I heard the most beautiful voice I had ever heard. No longer in the shadow of the valley of death, but right down in that valley, the nurse who gently wiped the final sweat beads from Matt's face began to sing. Yes, she sang. Songs of praise, songs of hope, songs of worship.

I wondered if this was how God felt when He watched *His* Son's body being prepared for burial. At no time in my life was the sacrifice of God the Father in redemption so poignant, so real, so painful, or so amazing. How could God just give up his Son willingly for me? For you? Just as that moment would have been the worst time to criticize my son to me, or to point out his faults; how can God still love this world so much when the world is so cold to Him, so unimpressed with his sacrifice? How could He love us so much? So much that He GAVE His only son. Matt (and Chris) was right. You really are great!

CHAPTER 21

Parting Is Such Sweet Sorrow

The private graveside will always be the most painful to me. It was a cool, but sunny March Tuesday morning. The hands of Matt's very young friends, along with those of my "Three Musketeers" would be the hands that carried the flawed shell that held my son on its final journey. Paul, my Pastor, spoke words that were eloquent, encouraging, uplifting, and kind all at the same time. The prayer was well versed, yet the overwhelming hopelessness lingered near. It must have felt the same way for God Himself, multiplied infinitely, on the day the soldiers rolled the stone over the mouth of the grave that held *His* Son.

We were surrounded by close friends and family outwardly, and held tightly by an army of angels inwardly. It was almost as if I could hear Christ emphatically say: "No one gets to my Children today." Oddly enough, though downtrodden, I recall feeling safer during those moments than I ever have at any other time in my life.

After leaving the graveside we all went to the house. Many of Matt's friends stopped by and left; others stopped by and stayed. Many shared stories, some that we had never heard.

With every passing moment, my spirit soared ever higher. I did not, and do not, understand it, but waiting for Matt's Celebration service that same evening seemed more like a child waiting for Christmas morning. It was as if I could sense that the very dynamics of my life were beginning to change.

I told no one that I had been working on a video for this service for weeks. Periodically I would close my office door, stack up a couple boxes of tissues and edit. For months now the volunteers in our Worship Ministry had carried the weight of their leader. This night would be no exception. I had a team assembled that agreed to lead in worship in Matt's honor. They agreed to do anything-- anything that is except mourn the dead. Matt lived 22 years. He was only sick 14 months. How foolish it would be to focus on such a small part of his existence.

The church was packed and the remote video venues were opened. The seats were full of members, friends, family, policemen, and firemen. Many of Matt's doctors, nurses, friends, college professors, and schoolteachers were there. There was a video countdown, the lights dimmed and the drummer kicked off the familiar rhythm for FRIEND OF GOD... and God rushed in. That evening Celebration included other videos, pictures, a stirring eulogy from Matt's Uncle Steve, and a great message from Matt's Pastor. But mostly it was about worship. We met for just a little over an hour that Tuesday evening, about the time of a typical worship service. At the end, it was time to use the video I had been working on.

While editing, I found some pretty rough videos of Matt leading a Worship Medley. We chose some of Matt's signature tunes for the end of the celebration service. With the magic of video and click tracks, Matt led our church in worship for one last time. The final tune? You guessed it, "How Great Is Our God." It was a rough audio mix, it needed some bass, a little drums and some texture. With scenes from Matt's life flashing across the large screens, his friends played and sang along live to fill in the missing parts. It seemed to us that Matt was carried into eternity on the wings of his favorite song... the same song he learned to play his guitar with only a precious few years earlier.

That celebration service did not heal our wounds. It did not bring us closure. It was not by any means a "cure all." But it was wonderful and it did teach me another valuable lesson. *If a child wishes to propel a plastic boat across a pond, it is best to begin by pointing it in the right direction and applying a firm shove.* That is exactly what that Tuesday night did for us. It framed Matt's death by the manner in which he lived, bringing glory to God. We had been overwhelmed with death. This evening painted Matt's death and suffering in the light of his life and its greater impact. I can't help but wonder: could this be a small piece of what God felt when the grave released His Son?

Some say the parting is a *sweet* sorrow. While I think I know what that means, in this situation there was nothing sweet about it. The guarantee of a reunion to come? Now that is truly sweet.

CHAPTER 22

The Greater Journey

It was two and a half years after Matt's memorial service that I had the opportunity to attend a Worship Pastor's Conference at Disney World. "Disney World?" you might ask. You bet! I have laughed with many people about this conference. When asked why I chose Disney as a place to attend such a conference, my answer is always the same: Because Paul (my boss) said "No" to the conference that was on a cruise ship. At any rate, I had the opportunity to attend.

Disney has long been known for its "magic." From the original pioneers, Walt and Roy, and simple animations that brought imagination to life, to today's state of the art music, fireworks, and special effects productions, the intent seems to be the same: to connect to the inner child, to give life to dreams and encourage imagination. When I learned that the cost of the conference included an evening at the "Magic Kingdom" I was elated! It seemed that on this evening several "A-team" Christian artists would perform during extended park hours.

During this same time in Texas, the summer of 2011, we experienced the hottest summer on record; along with the worst drought most old timers could ever remember. I guess that's why the prevalent afternoon thunderstorms of central Florida seemed almost an oddity. The worst of those from that week came—you guessed it—on Friday afternoon while we were riding a bus on the way to the park! When we exited the bus, no one dared make the trek from bus stop to entrance gate. It was a distance of several hundred yards, and with no cover.

The rain came down literally sideways at times, with lightning and thunder that was ominous in its tone. Several of the group migrated towards the center of the awning covering the bus stop area. Shaunda, being her meticulous, phlegmatic self, searched for any remaining dry concrete, took me by the hand and led me there. Amazing! It seemed to be the only place the windswept rain could not reach. As I laughed at her simple, yet profound wisdom, I noticed we had but one other person in our newly discovered haven.

It was a young man who joined us, rather thin and dressed all in black with longer black hair. I remembered him being on the same Disney transport bus from our resort. Most folks on that bus were from our conference, and I correctly assumed he was as well.

He was very friendly, and immediately struck up a conversation. He asked if I had been attending the conference, and specifically what I thought about the previous evening's message. He went on to share how at 28 years of age, he had already lived in 5 states. The message that evening had been about the great value of finding somewhere to minister and staying there long term. I told him that he was living proof that I was right in my initial conceptions of the conference attendees: I had been serving as a Worship Pastor (30 years at the time), two years longer than he had been alive. We both laughed, but I realized that it was because of my age that he was talking to me in the first place.

I glanced toward Shaunda, and found in her eyes the permission to go where I felt that God was prompting. "Going somewhere and staying," I said, "Yes, there is a lot to be said for that." At that time, I had already been working on this book for many months, and in no more than 3 minutes I shared with him the majority of the story of Matt. I told him that I had been at Family

Fellowship then for 17 years, and 15 years when my Son passed away.

I told him that my son had led worship right beside me for years, and that he was in his third year of Bible College, studying for the ministry. I told him the truth… that I have no idea how I would have ever made it through without my Church. Then as quickly as it started, as it so often does in Central Florida, the rain stopped.

And there it was. After two and one half years I was finally able to see Matt's story not only for what it *was*, but also for what it *could be*.

I looked at Shaunda and asked if she was ready to go into the park. When she said "yes," she smiled, but I could see small tears glistening in the corners of her eyes, as I'm certain they were in mine. When I acknowledged her, the young man I had been speaking with reached his hand towards her and said:

"I'm sorry; we didn't have a chance to meet. What is your name?"

My wife replied "Shaunda."

"Nice to meet you," the young gentleman said. "My name is Matt."

It seemed as if, for that one moment, all of time stood at attention. I grasped my wife's hand firmly as we walked underneath the gray sky to the entrance gates of the park. And in those few steps as I held Shaunda's hand tightly in mine, it was as if I could once again feel God's hand tightly holding my other.

If a work of animation can spin life into a wooden puppet or the touch of a fairy's wand could light a castle, why should we be surprised when a touch from the hand of God brings new life into a heart long dead?

As I promised in the beginning, this is not a work about recovery from grief. I have but one lifetime, and that is not nearly enough for this broken heart to fully recover. I have learned this much though. When you lose a child, large parts of your heart just die. It is as if the pain is so desperate and the heart hurts so dreadfully that it is easier not to feel at all, than to feel the pain.

I have also learned that *just as quickly as life leaves your heart as cold as stone, it can return;* much as the rain on a hot central Florida afternoon. In this reality I found hope in the midst of one of life's greatest losses.

I learned that no matter how painful, life without rain would leave our hearts and spirits as dry, cracked, and broken as the ground during that long hot summer in Texas. The healing hand of God is a power that defies description or explanation. Yet it is as real, and as necessary as the air we breathe. Even though as I write this, I feel the tears coming once again, I realize I have learned yet one more thing. I have learned to say, "*Thank you God...thank you for the rain.*"

I am still really at the beginning of my journey, but near the end of this work. I am also drawing ever nearer to the end of my career. These days I find myself praying more and more in one specific direction. God, may I please finish well.

Although the majority of my adventures lay behind, there still awaits one last adventure. I'd like to think that one day in the vast eternity that awaits, I might enjoy a special reunion. Perhaps it will take place in a golden field of grain, perhaps beside a quiet stream. I'd like to sit with Matt one more time and be sure he realizes that he gave me some of the best moments of my life. I'd even like Chris Tomlin to join us so I could tell him what his song has meant to my family. Who knows, we may even pass around a couple of acoustic guitars and join in a chorus or two of "How Great is Our God." After all, I know the words very well. I heard them over and over all those years ago. For even though it is quiet now, even in the quietest part of the night, I can still hear the song.

I remember the first time Shaunda and I went back to the place where we left Matt's body in the granite field that Tuesday morning. It was just a few days later. It was then that we first noticed that there were some items left there, presumably by the other kids. There was a plastic soft drink bottle of Matt's favorite drink along with a small toy truck. There was also a picture in a small frame;

it was that picture of the second Christmas taken at the house in front of the fireplace, when all the kids were together.

We still visit Matt's grave from time to time, but oddly enough I don't feel close to him there. That is still a place of sadness and finality. Besides, I don't have to go very far to feel close to Matt.

He is in my office at church where his guitars hang on either side of a Texas State Senate proclamation given in his honor. A Texas State Senator, my friend, wrote it and had it read on the floor of the Texas State Senate in honor of Matt's life.

He is still right beside me every week when I stand on our platform to lead worship. I can honestly say there has *never* been one Sunday that I have not thought of Matt.

It was here I learned another lesson. ***It is in special places that Matt's spirit is still very much alive***. He is most certainly not in a box covered with six feet of dirt.

I have done many things in my life of which I tend to be so proud of that the human side of me would love to display from a signpost. Then again, that same human side of me has done so many things that I would rather you didn't ever find out.

I chased "the dream" as a young man, but that chase ended somewhere on the lonely streets of music row. It's much different now, much quieter. Where I sit writing these words is on the bank of a picturesque river in a southeastern Oklahoma state park. The warm sun belies the fact that it is late winter and still well before the season. I can hear a variety of birds, but mostly I hear the gentle breeze blowing through the pine trees. The air is clean.

Long gone now are the dreams of becoming a great songwriter or performer. As such, there will be no manuscripts of this work submitted to publishers similar to what I used to do with my songs all those years ago. Thankfully, neither will there be any anxious days spent waiting, rewarded only by a rejection letter. As a matter of fact, I cannot even be certain that anyone will ever read these words. And that is fine by me. You see, the joy for me is no longer in hoping that someone of stature will validate my work. It is found rather in knowing that *the* person of stature validated my life through the sacrifice of His Son.

Today, I realize that I am a rich man not because I can spend a few days in a slightly dated state park Lodge catching the off-season rates. No, rather I am a rich man because I can write these words while staying at a slightly dated state park Lodge catching the off-season rates…and truly be at peace.

Now I am not totally unlearned, I know there are "cornfields" yet to come. But, I have also learned that *In spite of the past hurts, there may be adventures yet to come as well.* These days, as never before, I seem to be captivated by one prayer.

May I complete the remainder of my career...and my life...and somehow live a life that honors You. May I, as Your child, please You and make You proud, just as my son did me.

As difficult as this journey has been, may I remind you that I write not so I can forget, I write so I can remember. I write because I am afraid someday I will forget.

So many of the lessons I have learned have been profound, some so profound I had to learn them several times. Others were far more simple. One of the greatest that is perhaps both simple *and* profound is this:

What I remind you of here is not intended for shock value, so please don't misjudge me. Truth is, we are not supposed to worship God because He is good. Now don't misunderstand, God certainly *is* good, and He is good all the time. It's just this: there are times when He allows things to come into our lives where He does not *appear* to be good. To be brutally honest, there are times He seems unexplainably absent at best, and unbelievably cruel at worst. The Bible is not joking with us when it tells us that His ways and His thoughts are not ours. They are higher than ours. They are at times well beyond our ability to grasp or even reason away. And that is where faith must take over on our heart. Faith tells me that He still *is* good.

It is His very nature. After all, "God *is* love." Question is: "What do I *choose* to believe?" Do I trust Him or don't I?

On one particular Sunday morning Matt would teach me this, one of the most valuable lessons I have ever learned.

I don't know why God took Matt. Doesn't make any sense to me at all. It doesn't seem fair. On the outside it doesn't make God look like He is very "good" at all. If my worship is based on God's goodness, I have been provided a convenient back door, a way to check out of the whole thing if you will. The enemy wants you to run out that back door and declare that God never existed at all.

And there it is, staring me square in the face: "The *Greater* Journey," trusting God despite the pain. Believing there is a reason even when I cannot see it, or feel it.

No, we are not to worship God because He is *good*. We are to worship God because He is *God*. This *is* the "Greater Journey."

So to you, Matt, thanks for teaching me the deepest lesson of all about life. ***I must be willing to leave all of life behind with grace, dignity and honor to Christ***. I pray I have learned it well, for I, like everyone else, will face the same Journey; and I, like you, will have to face it alone.

And, oh yeah, one great and final lesson that I learned, at least to this point that is. (It seems like there may be more to come.) That lesson is simple; *no matter how bad things are, they could always be worse*.

"Worse?" I think I just heard someone ask. "What could be worse than losing a child?" I have an answer for that, and it really is quite simple, and it is unimaginably worse. What is worse than losing a child? Losing a child and not being certain of where that child will spend eternity.

You see, after all the heartache, the tears, the pain, the unspeakable pain, I know, based on Matt's words backed up by the way he lived as well as the way he died, that Matt today is in a place where there is no more pain. The earthly body that failed him is now replaced by a glorified body that knows no suffering.

Because of the immeasurable sacrifice of Christ on the cross, Matt no longer struggles to breathe; his lungs are full of heaven's breezes.

Because there was a time that Matt asked Christ to come into his heart and forgive his sins, he no longer exists in an atmosphere clouded by suffering and questions. Instead he "knows as he is known." And unlike all of us who remain here, he has no questions that remain unanswered. Heaven has no city named "Whyville."

Through it all, I never one time saw Matt cry, although he surely must have. Now he lives in a land where there are no more tears.

As for me, I have cried more tears more times than I would ever care to admit. It seemed that every tear was in some respect a question of trust: that sometimes-daily decision of whether I would trust God or not. The choice I faced in the surgery waiting room on that cold Christmas Eve morning so many years ago.

With every tear I shed I would tell God that I still trusted Him, it's just that my human side is so weak. A while back, if you recall, I began to imagine that I was collecting all of those tears. I was placing those tears, as it were, in a small brown bottle that would fit in my shirt pocket. When I would finish crying, I would place a cork in the top of the bottle to preserve my tears for a day yet to come.

My son Matt cannot come back to me; and what's more, he wouldn't even if he could. But I, like King David said when he lost his son, can go to him, and one day I will. With this future day in mind, I play the following scenario out in my head over and over.

Sometimes when I dream I imagine nearing heaven's gate and finding Matt there to meet me. We share an extended man-to-man bear hug that would be the envy of any reunion. After a few moments, and a few hallelujahs, I reach into my shirt pocket and retrieve the bottle, the bottle full of my tears. Now we all know there is no place for tears in this land.

It is then that I imagine approaching my Savior, small brown bottle in hand. I fall on my knees as I near the Holy One into Whose presence I am not worthy to enter. I realize that despite my failures, struggles, and questions I am in the presence of Jesus Himself, and only by His grace.

I raise the bottle, remove the cork and pour my tears at His feet as an offering.

Then and there I, too, will be free of the struggles, the doubts, the questions... and the tears. No longer in need of a container to catch any more tears, I think I'll just toss the small, brown, empty bottle into the river of life.

As it drifts off into eternity, Matt and I might then take a while to catch up, and then maybe take a walk, arms around each other's shoulders, on into eternity.

CHAPTER 23

The Last Words

I am now writing the final words for this book. Please don't misunderstand, there are some elements to follow, but these are the last words to be recorded in this journal.

I am finishing up in my office at Church. It is a great space, although many of my "friends" question if it is an office at all. They consider it more of a playroom. I am surrounded by computers, screens, monitors and keyboards flanked by a vocal booth on my left (maybe "they" are correct after all). To my right is a full cup of coffee held in my "Route 66" cup that I purchased on a recent pilgrimage down the "Mother Road." We have enjoyed an early spring in Texas and it is quite warm for this time of the year. To put it another way, today is a good day.

And then again it's not. For you see, today is March 15, and this is the anniversary of Matt's death.

When I reach the end of the street that leaves my small subdivision I am faced with a choice. Either way I turn can take me to the Church. They are both nearly equal in distance. A right turn takes me west and through our small city. A left turn takes me east and is a more scenic drive. Unfortunately it also takes me past the granite field. You might be surprised how many mornings (including this one) that I consider that final fact before I turn. Today I went left.

As soon as my truck completed the turn I was facing east, and I was greeted by a beautiful East Texas sunrise. The sun had already fled the horizon, but was just now rising above the cloud cover displaying sharply defined rays of light streaking in multiple directions. It was more than I could resist. I grabbed my phone and took a picture.

Just then I passed the granite field. I glanced to the left at the seemingly endless rows of markers; then back to the right where the sunrise once again filled my peripheral vision. Without a conscious decision I looked again to the left and back to the right.

My next thought was that what I had just experienced was really just a picture of the journey; hopelessness and sadness one second, hope and beauty the next.

But then I realized that I only experienced both on this morning because I turned left instead of right. Had I made the other decision I would have driven through traffic and past retail shops. I would have merged onto the Interstate and no doubt accelerated to highway speeds where most of the surroundings become an indeterminate blur. I would have missed both experiences. They are also inexorably linked.

The last words? "Yes" and "yes."

"Yes," God can be trusted. He is faithful beyond anything I could ever imagine. He has been the singular unifying presence in my life. People come and go. Jobs come and go. Possessions come and go. Even children come and go. Christ, on the other hand, came and stayed.

And "yes," I am, at least so far, trusting Him. I cannot speak for the future; I can only live one day at a time. I have learned on at least two occasions now that there are emotions I cannot handle. There are circumstances I cannot get through. And thanks to a journey through the cornfield, I also realize that I serve a God who is threatened by neither.

He can be trusted, and He has never once left my side. Keep in mind, God is still God. *He* will have the last word.

A Certain Sorrow

Several months ago now my wife and I were preparing for a quick vacation. This time it was Shaunda who was up at the crack of dawn and was ready to leave long before I was. It is great to see her smile again.

Lauren has a new love interest. They come by our house. The four of us go out and eat. We have a great time. I don't know if he's the "one" or not, but one thing is certain though. I'll feel sorry for whatever poor guy it is when it comes the time to ask for Lauren's hand. He's got a surprise coming. In addition to merely asking Lauren's fine dad for permission to marry, there's one extra stop he needs to make! I'm not sure at all what I'll tell whomever it is that asks, but one thing is for sure... I'll make sure he knows that Lauren is no "Jenny," (sorry Forrest!). I assure you, this girl knows what love is.

Sometimes life's journey provides interesting dichotomies. For example, this journey has not been good, nor will I ever say that it was a good thing; yet so much good has come from it. From where I stand today I can honestly say I would not go through it again for a million dollars; nor would I take a million dollars in exchange for what I have learned.

All of the rest of us talk more these days; I guess none of us takes much for granted any more. I have a perfect Granddaughter (ok, that part's not even close to true. She's spoiled rotten...and I did my part). She thinks I'm special... and I know she is!

A couple of years ago, Brian, our youngest, decided he would "be all that he could be." A couple of months ago we had a going away family get together in his honor before he took off for Afghanistan. It was actually a wonderful few days for me. We laughed, ate, talked, ate, went to the Texas State Fair, remembered Matt, ate, shared stories... you get the picture. And all of us were together. And I didn't take one moment for granted. I would venture to say that no one else did either.

Maybe that's one of the final lessons, at least before I finish this book. *Never take one moment of life for granted.*

Life's pace has picked up. I look at the calendar more often these days than I do the clock. I will also admit that there is a large open field down the road from our home. The one landscaped with granite. It contains a myriad of painful memories for me, and the remains of the broken human shell that held Matt.

Sure we've moved on, at least a bit. But I must admit that nearly every time Shaunda and I drive by that field, our eyes, and our hearts inevitably and inexplicably turn that way. I guess there will always be a certain sorrow in that place. But it also reminds me of the greatest lesson of all. This one brings with it great hope! *Because of the sacrifice of another Son, my son is not in the grave at all.*

God willingly sacrificed *His* son Jesus to make the way for my Son Matt to spend eternity in heaven. You see, the "good" in Matt was not really the "good in Matt" at all. It rather was the reflection of the Great Son lived out through a great son. My prayer for you as you finish this book is the same prayer Matt would share if he could.

If you do not know the greatest love that was ever known, take a moment and meet Christ. You will then one day understand the truth of the scripture that teaches us that the troubles in this world are not even worthy to be compared to the glory in the world yet to come.

> *That is why we never give up. Though our bodies are dying, our spirits are being renewed every day. For our present troubles are small and won't last very long. Yet they produce for us a glory that vastly outweighs them and will last forever! So we don't look at the troubles we can see now; rather, we fix our gaze on things that cannot be seen. For the things we see now will soon be gone, but the things we cannot see will last forever. (2 Corinthians 4:16-18)*

For you see, this world is not really about this world at all. This world is about the next one.

CHAPTER 24
The Unthinkable

A MESSAGE FROM MATT'S MOM (SHAUNDA)

Well into our present journey we had the opportunity to tell Matt's story at a beautiful church in Eureka Springs, Arkansas. The Pastor, who is a licensed psychologist, is a longtime friend of Joe's. It was a real blessing to watch him and Joe reconnect after being separated for many years.

After the services the four of us had the chance to spend some real time together. This Pastor's wife is a wonderful person and is a credit to Pastor's wives everywhere. We sat down in their home after church, where I was introduced to the game of Rook, and introduced to chips, dips, and more desserts than you can imagine. Talk about the perfect evening!

Tongue in cheek, Joe cautioned me ahead of time to keep an eye on this man. With Joe's warning that he was a "real psychologist," he told me not to answer any questions that began with the words "How do you feel about...." The question he asked me didn't start like that, so I was blindsided.

Without warning, he looked right at me and said: "I understand what Joe is trying to get across to people when he speaks of Matt, but what do you hope people will learn from Matt's story?

"Wow," was all I could think. "Pass the brownies," was all I could say. It was a great question, and one that really forced me to think. Joe is the speaker, the singer, and the writer. I handle the computer and talk to people...privately. Not, like, up in front.

Here was the answer that I gave that night. I think it surprised even Joe. I hope it helps and encourages you. If you are a mother or grandmother, I pray it challenges you as well.

Here is one of the greatest lessons I learned. When Joe tells Matt's story, he usually includes the part about Matt being a great athlete, and truly he was. To illustrate that point, Joe usually tells people that he "has the home run balls to prove it." We really do still have quite a few, but not as many as we used to. Each of the kids took some, but there are several left.

In the corner of a closet I have a small wooden box. I call it my "Matt box." In it are some pictures, a few of Matt's personal effects, some of his achievement certificates and awards…and a baseball. I was looking at these things one day when I was all by myself. When I held that baseball in my hand I realized a very important truth: when a person dies, they really don't take anything with them. Nothing. No trophies or awards. And certainly no baseballs.

The only thing that I ever had a part in giving Matt that he did take with him was Christ. The most important thing we can "give" our kids is to introduce them to the Lord. If the unthinkable happens in your home as it did in mine, they won't take with them a single "Straight A" report card, academic or sport's trophy. It's not up to us to save our kids, but it assuredly is our responsibility to introduce them to Christ, to take them to church, and to make spiritual things a priority in their lives. A priority over sporting events or scholastic meets. You never know when they go to church camp, Sunday school, or a youth activity, if it will be the real life changer for them.

If you had asked me ten years ago, I would have told you this would never happen to any of our kids. They were all healthy. But how quickly that can change. If I were sitting across the couch from a young mom right now I would tell them to make Christ the single priority of their life. Words are important, actions are much more important. A child learns from seeing more than from hearing. If I wish for my child to make Christ a priority in their life, I must make Him the priority of mine.

Translated, that means instead of heading to the lake for some fishing, or going golfing, to the movies, or just lying in bed on Sunday morning, get up and take your children to Church. Put down that secular novel and allow your children to catch you reading your Bible, every day. Turn off your favorite radio station and fill your home and your car with Christian music.

There is certainly nothing wrong with softball, baseball, or most other activities. They can be good for your kids. Likewise there is nothing necessarily wrong with Pilates, yoga, workouts, or a good pedicure. These can be good for you. There exists however, a grave danger when we allow busyness to fill our lives to the place where we worry more about running an efficient taxi service than providing a godly home. It's OK to say no to any activity if that is the path that leads to your child saying yes to God. Slow down, breathe, and hold your children close. We have no guarantee we will even be able to do that tomorrow.

Today I am grateful that I have an old battered baseball to hold in my hand and a box full of awards to look at. I am unbelievably more grateful that I have the assurance that Matt is in Heaven with Christ. The next time you face one of these "priority decisions" with your children, or for you, put yourself in circumstances similar to mine. Here's the lesson: ***Make decisions you will wish you had should this unthinkable tragedy visit your home.***

Closing thoughts…

So there it is, the story that so profoundly changed our lives. Now I'll bet you understand why it was so easy for Shaunda and I to set out on our "present journey."

In March of 2016, seven years after Matt's death and after twenty-one years of service to my church, we sold our home, most of our possessions, and purchased a pickup truck and a fifth wheel we lovingly named "The Virge," in honor of Matt. We have now invested our lives in telling Matt's story through speaking, music, and video in a one-hour presentation entitled "The Greater Journey Live Worship Event." Our ministry plan calls us to "share

Matt's incredible story of hope anytime, anywhere, with no mention of finances."

Is the message of Matt's story something that would speak to the hearts of people you know or serve? Let's start a conversation about bringing this life-changing story to your Church, organization, or conference.

www.joeknight.us

The Lessons...

- *Time is relative to the event.*

- *There are places that your kids have to go that you just can't go with them.*

- *The darkest journey is made a little easier with the help of fellow travelers.*

- *Our sovereign God sometimes chooses paths for us that may hold pain, disappointment and loss.*

- *What will be will be. The only question is, "Will I trust God or will I not?"*

- *There are those who will choose to take the journey with us at great cost to themselves.*

- *There is a part of every journey that has to be experienced alone.*

- *Honest unselfish love gives even when there is little hope of return.*

- *God is big enough for my questions.*

- *These lessons He is teaching me come straight from His broken heart.*

- *Despair is the polar opposite of faith.*

- *Filling your life with busyness does not make reality go away.*

- *Hope is as powerful as a drug, and just as addictive.*

- *Despair is a cruel master.*

- *Be quiet and just listen.*

- *There are things we can experience in this life that are far worse than death.*

- *We don't worship God because He is good, we worship God because He is God*

- *Sometimes there can be a million reasons to make a right decision, but it has nothing to do with a dollar.*

- *If a child wishes to propel a plastic boat across a pond, it is best to begin by pointing it in the right direction and applying a firm shove.*

- *Just as quickly as life leaves your heart as cold as stone, it can return.*

- *"Thank you, God...thank you for the rain."*

- *It is in special places that Matt's spirit is still very much alive.*

- *I must be willing to leave all of life behind with grace, dignity and honor to Christ.*

- *No matter how bad things are, they could always be worse.*

- *Never take one moment of life for granted.*

- *Because of the sacrifice of another Son, my son is not in the grave at all.*

- *Make decisions you will wish you had should this unthinkable tragedy visit your home.*

> Then I heard a sweet voice calling.
> Look around, you're not far from home.
> I'm big enough for all your questions
> And you've never walked alone.

www.ingramcontent.com/pod-product-compliance
Lightning Source LLC
LaVergne TN
LVHW052024080426
835513LV00018B/2136